THE STATES AND THE NATION SERIES, of which this volume is a part, is designed to assist the American people in a serious look at the ideals they have espoused and the experiences they have undergone in the history of the nation. The content of every volume represents the scholarship, experience, and opinions of its author. The costs of writing and editing were met mainly by grants from the National Endowment for the Humanities, a federal agency. The project was administered by the American Association for State and Local History, a nonprofit learned society, working with an Editorial Board of distinguished editors, authors, and historians, whose names are listed below.

EDITORIAL ADVISORY BOARD

James Morton Smith, General Editor
Director, State Historical Society
of Wisconsin

William T. Alderson, Director
American Association for
State and Local History

Roscoe C. Born
Vice-Editor
The National Observer

Vernon Carstensen
Professor of History
University of Washington

Michael Kammen, Professor of
American History and Culture
Cornell University

Louis L. Tucker
President (1972–1974)
American Association for
State and Local History

Joan Paterson Kerr
Consulting Editor
American Heritage

Richard M. Ketchum
Editor and Author
Dorset, Vermont

A. Russell Mortensen
Assistant Director
National Park Service

Lawrence W. Towner
Director and Librarian
The Newberry Library

Richmond D. Williams
President (1974–1976)
American Association for
State and Local History

MANAGING EDITOR

Gerald George
American Association for
State and Local History

Alaska

A Bicentennial History

William R. Hunt

W. W. Norton & Company, Inc.
New York

American Association for State and Local History
Nashville

Author and publishers make grateful acknowledgment to the following for permission to quote from archival materials and previously published works:

The Archives, the University of Alaska, for permission to quote from the Pilcher Collection and the Van Valin Collection.

Director, the Bancroft Library, the University of California at Berkeley, for permission to quote from "Papers Relating to an Investigation of Charges of Sorcery."

Alaska Magazine, for permission to quote from the "Letters" section of *Alaska Magazine,* issues dated April, November, and December 1973. Copyright © 1973, the Alaska Northwest Publishing Company.

The Alaska Journal, for permission to quote from "A Conference with the Tanana Chiefs," by Stanton H. Patty, which appeared in the *Alaska Journal* (Spring 1971). Copyright © 1971, *The Alaska Journal.*

The *Polar Record,* for permission to quote from "Off-Shore Oil and Gas Developments in Alaska: Impacts and Conflicts," by George W. Rogers, which appeared in the *Polar Record* 17, no. 108 (1974). Copyright © 1974, the Scott Polar Research Institute.

The *Western Historical Quarterly,* for permission to quote from "The Canoe Rocks— We Do Not Know What Will Become of Us," by Ted C. Hinckley, which appeared in the *Western Historical Quarterly* 1 (July 1970). Copyright © 1970, the *Western Historica, Quarterly,* Utah State University.

Maurice R. Montgomery, for permission to quote from "An Arctic Murder" (Master's thesis, University of Oregon, 1963).

Bobby Lain, for permission to quote from *North of Fifty-Three* (Ann Arbor: University Microfilms, 1974).

Library of Congress Cataloging in Publication Data

Hunt, William R
    Alaska, a Bicentennial history.

    (The States and the Nation series)
    Bibliography: p.
    Includes index.
    1. Alaska—History. I. Title. II. Series.
F904.H84   979.8   76–44422
ISBN 0–393–05604–X

Published and distributed by W. W. Norton & Company, Inc.
500 Fifth Avenue
New York, New York 10036

Printed in the United States of America

1 2 3 4 5 6 7 8 9 0

To the memory of Fabian Carey, Alaskan trapper,
and the pioneers of the state

Contents

Illustrations

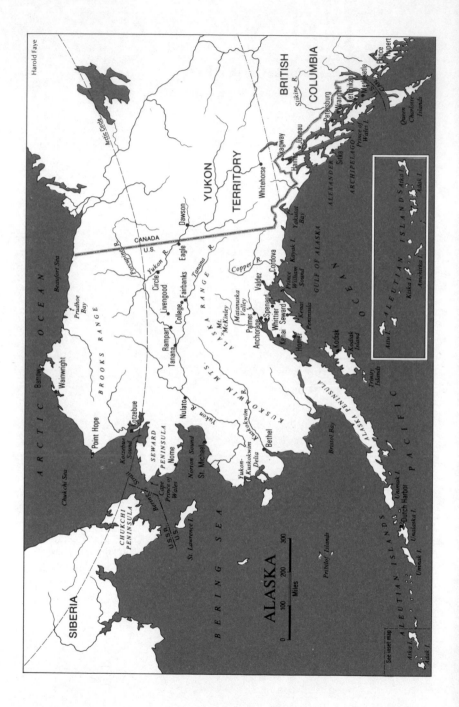

Harold Faye

Invitation to the Reader

IN 1807, former President John Adams argued that a complete history of the American Revolution could not be written until the history of change in each state was known, because the principles of the Revolution were as various as the states that went through it. Two hundred years after the Declaration of Independence, the American nation has spread over a continent and beyond. The states have grown in number from thirteen to fifty. And democratic principles have been interpreted differently in every one of them.

We therefore invite you to consider that the history of your state may have more to do with the bicentennial review of the American Revolution than does the story of Bunker Hill or Valley Forge. The Revolution has continued as Americans extended liberty and democracy over a vast territory. John Adams was right: the states are part of that story, and the story is incomplete without an account of their diversity.

The Declaration of Independence stressed life, liberty, and the pursuit of happiness; accordingly, it shattered the notion of holding new territories in the subordinate status of colonies. The Northwest Ordinance of 1787 set forth a procedure for new states to enter the Union on an equal footing with the old. The Federal Constitution shortly confirmed this novel means of building a nation out of equal states. The step-by-step process through which territories have achieved self-government and national representation is among the most important of the Founding Fathers' legacies.

The method of state-making reconciled the ancient conflict between liberty and empire, resulting in what Thomas Jefferson called an empire for liberty. The system has worked and remains unaltered, despite enormous changes that have taken

place in the nation. The country's extent and variety now sur-
pass anything the patriots of '76 could likely have imagined.
The United States has changed from an agrarian republic into a
highly industrial and urban democracy, from a fledgling nation
into a major world power. As Oliver Wendell Holmes remarked
in 1920, the creators of the nation could not have seen com-
pletely how it and its constitution and its states would develop.
Any meaningful review in the bicentennial era must consider
what the country has become, as well as what it was.

The new nation of equal states took as its motto *E Pluribus
Unum*—"out of many, one." But just as many peoples have
become Americans without complete loss of ethnic and cultural
identities, so have the states retained differences of character.
Some have been superficial, expressed in stereotyped images—
big, boastful Texas, "sophisticated" New York, "hillbilly"
Arkansas. Other differences have been more real, sometimes instructively, sometimes amusingly; democracy has embraced
Huey Long's Louisiana, bilingual New Mexico, unicameral Nebraska, and a Texas that once taxed fortunetellers and spawned
politicians called "Woodpecker Republicans" and "Skunk
Democrats." Some differences have been profound, as when
South Carolina secessionists led other states out of the Union in
opposition to abolitionists in Massachusetts and Ohio. The result was a bitter Civil War.

The Revolution's first shots may have sounded in Lexington
and Concord; but fights over what democracy should mean and
who should have independence have erupted from Pennsylvania's Gettysburg to the "Bleeding Kansas" of John Brown,
from the Alamo in Texas to the Indian battles at Montana's
Little Bighorn. Utah Mormons have known the strain of isolation; Hawaiians at Pearl Harbor, the terror of attack; Georgians
during Sherman's march, the sadness of defeat and devastation.
Each state's experience differs instructively; each adds understanding to the whole.

The purpose of this series of books is to make that kind of understanding accessible, in a way that will last in value far
beyond the bicentennial fireworks. The series offers a volume
on every state, plus the District of Columbia—fifty-one, in all.

Each book contains, besides the text, a view of the state through eyes other than the author's—a "photographer's essay," in which a skilled photographer presents his own personal perceptions of the state's contemporary flavor.

We have asked authors not for comprehensive chronicles, nor for research monographs or new data for scholars. Bibliographies and footnotes are minimal. We have asked each author for a summing up—interpretive, sensitive, thoughtful, individual, even personal—of what seems significant about his or her state's history. What distinguishes it? What has mattered about it, to its own people and to the rest of the nation? What has it come to now?

To interpret the states in all their variety, we have sought a variety of backgrounds in authors themselves and have encouraged variety in the approaches they take. They have in common only these things: historical knowledge, writing skill, and strong personal feelings about a particular state. Each has wide latitude for the use of the short space. And if each succeeds, it will be by offering you, in your capacity as a *citizen* of a state *and* of a nation, stimulating insights to test against your own.

James Morton Smith
General Editor

Preface

*N*OT many spectators were present in Sitka on October 18, 1867, to watch the ceremony in which Russia formally transferred its North American possession to the United States. Aside from the American and Russian military, a handful of entrepreneurs from San Francisco and a few Sitkans, Russians, Indians, and Creoles looked on. Lowering the Russian flag and replacing it with the Stars and Stripes was not a difficult maneuver; but, even so, the commanders were chagrined to see it bungled. For some reason, the Russian flag refused to come down. It was embarrassing to the officials and a bore to most of the spectators. But it was the last straw for Maria Maksutova, the young wife of the retiring governor. The strain was too much for her, and she fainted dead away as a sailor was hoisted aloft to cut down the recalcitrant flag.

A cynic might discover in the flag incident on the day of the transfer of sovereignty the key to the history of the region for the next hundred-odd years. There were to be many instances of governmental bungling, and the ensuing strain would cause Alaskans, if not to faint, to scream with rage against their tormentors. Whether in the period of Russian rule or of American, battles with outside authority and complaints of government bungling and neglect have been central and recurrent in Alaska's story.

There have been many issues in Alaska's history, of course.

Among them, the struggles for self-government and for an economic base stand out. Alaskans did not achieve self-government easily. And exploitation of the resources of the land and the adjacent sea has always been hampered by the vast expanse of Alaska, by its remoteness from other states, and by the severe climate of most of the region. In the essay that follows, questions are raised. Did the people live in a way notably different from that of other Americans? How did the federal government treat Alaskans? Did attitudes of Alaskans differ from those of other Americans? How should the Alaskan experience be interpreted? Have Americans elsewhere viewed Alaska in a realistic or a romantic way? And what of Alaskans' own conception of their lands and lives: how much myth and self-deception does it exhibit? However, a short essay can only seek to consider rather than to answer definitively questions as complex as those.

In dealing with such matters, a writer of Alaskan history can easily be overwhelmed by the vast land itself and be tempted to treat it and its people romantically. In broad, colorful strokes, he might paint parka-clad sourdoughs and Eskimo hunters of marine mammals. The land's towering mountains, grinding glaciers, great forests, and rivers certainly inspire awe. Yet, if one reflects on Alaska's past, another vision supplants that of nature's wonders. The scene that intrudes is that of a congressional hearing room in Washington. There the air is not brisk and clear, as it is in most of Alaska; it is smoky and heated by disputation. But this room indeed has had as much significance for the development of Alaska as the physical features of the land. Within the walls of countless committee rooms, legislators have determined the policies that would govern Alaska and control the unplumbed resources of that vast land.

ACKNOWLEDGMENTS

I am pleased to thank the administration of the University of Alaska for aiding me in this project, in particular, Dr. Charles Ray, Dr. Richard Solie, Dr. Earl Beistline, and President Robert Hiatt.

A brilliant group of women typed and retyped this manuscript, performing with speed and good cheer even when my longhand script dissipated into vague squiggles. My deep thanks to Kathleen Aamodt, Mary Hayes, Judy Stephenson, and Barbara White—and to Dr. Robert Carlson, Director of the university's Institute of Water Resources, who gave staff support to this work.

I asked a number of people what they felt should be encompassed in an "interpretative essay" such as this. In particular, Dr. Claus-M. Naske, a specialist in Alaskan history at the university, offered ideas, suggested themes, and read the manuscript carefully on three separate occasions. Good editors are essential. Gerald George must be one of the best.

As always, my wife helped me out with skillful copy editing, suggestions, and encouragement.

June 1976   *William R. Hunt*

Alaska

1

Top of the World: Paradox

N 1917, Sandy Smith, a far-ranging gold prospector who had participated in most of the northern stampedes, made a grueling journey from the interior of Alaska to the Arctic shore. Traveling with a partner, Smith went over the Brooks Range to the shore by boat. The pair spent as much time hauling the boat as voyaging in it. They had a sled and seven dogs, and once on the coast, they mushed for Point Barrow. Before much of the journey had been made, Smith stumbled into a mucky lake up to his knees. He managed to pull himself free and then discovered that he had been floundering in a reservoir of oil seepage. Smith went on to Barrow, but he did not forget the location of his find. Later, in New York, he interested the Standard Oil Company in petroleum prospects and was commissioned to lead a party of geologists to the oil lakes.

Smith and his party took the first ship sailing from Seattle to Nome in 1921—the venerable old Cunarder, *Victoria*—with great expectations. Life and conversation among old-time Alaskans aboard the *Victoria* was always easy, and secrets could not be kept. Soon the news was out that a geological party from a rival oil company was aboard, and their intent paralleled Smith's. Once ashore at Nome, both parties scrambled to charter schooners for the voyage to the Arctic Ocean. Smith got the *Silver Wave,* and his rivals secured the *Teddy Bear.* Both vessels were skippered by skilled Arctic navigators; none-

3

theless, they were stopped by the ice more than one hundred miles from their goal. Smith unloaded provisions and equipment and bought a skin boat from Eskimos to continue his journey. Twenty-five days after leaving Nome, he and his party reached the lakes ahead of their rivals and pounded in their stakes. It was a great effort, but to no purpose: in 1923, President Warren G. Harding established Naval Petroleum Reserve No. 4 around Smith's claims.

Sandy Smith's experience illustrates the enduring paradox of Alaskan history. Economic and political forces have been much more dominant than the lifestyles of particular individuals. And yet, in large part, individuals have made Alaska the distinct and unusual state that it is.

The names of the first people to inhabit Alaska are unknown to us. We can imagine the type of people they were: the fur-clad hunters stalking their animal prey across the Bering Sea land bridge; then they or their ancestors moving on to populate other parts of Alaska and the Americas. Some of their ancestors eventually moved to the Aleutians, where they made contact with other, later visitors from across the Bering Sea. These rough characters crossing from Siberia in the 1740s possessed little civility, but they knew what they wanted—shiploads of sea-otter skins and Aleut women with whom to bed down. The first Russians remained in Alaska only long enough to gather pelts; later, others stayed on and reared families of mixed blood and formed a curious union of mutually dependent people.

Then Europeans and Americans voyaged from the south to the land of the Aleuts, Eskimos, and Indians. John Ledyard was the first nonnative American to see Alaska. Ledyard, a dropout from Dartmouth College, sailed with Captain James Cook on his great voyage to Alaskan waters and celebrated America's defiance of Britain by deserting from the Royal Navy in 1776 before signing on with Cook as a corporal of marines. Ledyard's published narrative of his voyage attracted New England traders to the Northwest coast in quest of sea-otter furs.

After Ledyard's time, certain colorful figures appear in the transition between the old and the contemporary Alaska. The impact of these individuals, with their idiosyncrasies and strange experiences, remained incomplete. But recalling their history imparts a certain flavor to the times in which they lived.

Father Feodor Bashmakoff, for example, was an Eskimo who was ordained a Russian Orthodox priest in 1827. His unusual position as the sharer of two totally different traditions led him into an unfortunate attempt to merge customs of both. Poor Bashmakoff desecrated "an orthodox shrine by dipping pagan charms, such as sorcerers sell to the benighted natives, into the holy water blessed by the benediction of a priest and receiving payment in skins from the pagan natives for such sacrilegious action." His bishop let Bashmakoff off lightly, observing that the man "sinned more from ignorance than from malice or wickedness." [1]

Others who encountered the frustrations of life in the new frontier finally gave up and left. Thomas G. Murphy, for instance, edited Sitka's first newspaper in 1867. He joined with William Sumner Dodge, an early booster, in establishing a city government in Alaska. Murphy was Sitka's first city attorney— appointed by Mayor Dodge. As described by a friend, Murphy seemed just the type to succeed on the frontier:

> a politician, lawyer, priest, editor, printer, author and poet. . . . Gentle, jovial, full of story, bubbling with an excess of the product of the Blarney-stone, he was everywhere, knew everything, and was first and foremost to execute all things. He was the exuberant, irrepressible spirit of the country. Strongly imaginative, full of faith and hope, possessed of an organ of self-esteem that knew no abasement, he leaped at once to the front of events and astonished all with ideas he advanced, the schemes he proposed and the strategy he displayed in their execution. [2]

And yet Murphy, along with Dodge, grew discouraged and left. Their frustrations arose from their inability to get the federal government to provide land-title grants. The two men also found it hard to make a living in Alaska. Murphy took his paper to Seattle, and Dodge moved to San Diego.

1. "Papers Relating to an Investigation of Charges of Sorcery," p. 2 and p. 14, Bancroft Library, University of California, Berkeley, California.

2. Ted C. Hinckley, *The Americanization of Alaska, 1867–1897* (Palo Alto: Pacific Books, Publishers, 1972), p. 40.

Another colorful Alaskan who failed was Ivan Petrov, who took the first census in 1880 after having deserted from the U.S. Army several times. Petrov described the contrasts of the territory, the fertile valleys, which he reckoned might support millions of farmers, and the dreary Bering Sea coast inhabited by seal and walrus hunters, who have eked out a living there.[3] Petrov faltered in a manner similar to Father Bashmakoff. He embarrassed federal officials by turning over false translations of Russian documents for use in the diplomatic squabble over the Bering Sea fur seals—and accordingly lost his job.

Yet thousands flocked to the North after the discovery of gold on the Yukon River and the Seward Peninsula. A few grew rich and carried their wealth outside. Most left the country as poor as they arrived—but treasured the memory of their exciting experiences. Others overcame the country's many challenges and stayed to build permanent communities. Men like James and Richard Geoghegan prospected, operated roadhouses on the Valdez Trail, clerked for the federal court in Fairbanks, and hunted game for hungry miners. Richard Geoghegan enhanced the cultural level of Fairbanks by his presence. He mastered Arabic, Chinese, Hebrew, and approximately a hundred other languages, and translated an Aleut dictionary from the Russian.

George M. Pilcher, another '98er, settled on the lower Yukon and also succeeded. He traded with natives and chopped wood for the steamboats plying the river. He lived a serene life except for an annual spree in Nome, from which he would return gratefully with a heavy head. After a long life on the Yukon, Pilcher looked back with contentment: "I came to this Alaska a young man full of energy, industry, and a will to win. I am now well into my 67th year and can feel the tug of time. I have failed to win wealth but have maintained my self-respect and am convinced that I hold the respect of all—or most all—others. This is worth more than gold." [4]

A woman like Cornelia Noble would not have been able to

3. Ivan Petrov, *Report on the Population, Industries, and Resources of Alaska* (Washington, D.C.: Government Printing Office, 1884).

4. Diary of George M. Pilcher, December 31, 1930, Pilcher Collection, Archives, University of Alaska, Fairbanks, Alaska.

share Pilcher's enthusiasm. Miss Noble moved to Nome in 1903 to work as a stenographer. She neither earned a fortune nor discovered peace of mind. Rather, she fell ill, could not work, and in her despondency, killed herself. Yet a Seattle newspaper conjured up the romantic tale that she had taken her life because she had won an immense fortune in Nome and had recklessly squandered it.

William Van Valin, a teacher at the Arctic village of Wainwright, did, in fact, seek his fortune in Alaska. In 1914, having heard a report of an oil lake, Van Valin hitched up his reindeer and made a five-hundred-mile trip to investigate. He could smell the substance when he got within a mile of the site; then finally it came within view: "The sight that filled my eyes was most gratifying indeed. Two living springs of what appears like engine oil with their black beds winding over and down the hill." [5]

He very quickly staked a claim that included the hill from which the streams oozed and the good-sized lake, four hundred by two hundred feet, into which they drained. Van Valin noticed that the lake acted as a death trap for fowl and animals careless enough to mistake the oil for water and assumed that the lake bed might contain prehistoric fossils.

Mining regulations of the day required that a claim occupant do at least two hundred dollars' worth of work at the location to hold title to the site, so the teacher made plans to return the next summer and erect a house. But all he had time to do on that journey was to put his stakes out and raise a sign naming the place the "Arctic Rim Mineral Oil Claim."

Whether Van Valin ever did anything more about his claim beyond filling out the necessary documents is not clear from his diaries. His property was on the east side of Smith Bay about one mile from the Arctic shore and, since it is part of the U.S. Navy Reserve, it has not yet been drilled. Like Sandy Smith, Van Valin made a good start but left an incomplete record of his search for riches.

These individuals were struggling against more than the un-

5. Diary of William Van Valin, May 21, 1914, Van Valin Collection, Archives, University of Alaska, Fairbanks, Alaska.

predictable whims of government, however. They waged their personal dramas against a natural background so vast and rich that hyperbole comes almost too easily in describing it. When Secretary of State William H. Seward negotiated the purchase of Alaska from Russia, he brought within the orbit of the United States a territory larger than the combined areas of Washington, Oregon, California, Idaho, Nevada, and Utah—586,400 square miles. Alaska's shoreline is more than 31,000 miles long, far longer than that of any other state and greater than the shore-lines of the entire Eastern seaboard. The Alaskan continental shelf comprises 60 percent of the total North American shelf. And North America's highest mountain—Mount McKinley—pierces the sky at 20,320 feet, with eighteen other Alaskan peaks higher than 14,000 feet.

The true diversity of the state's geography is revealed in a survey of the six geographic regions. The rainfall in the Pan-handle, in the southeast, sometimes reaches two hundred inches a year—higher than that of some rain forests. And yet the weather is quite mild, differing notoriously from the cold tem-peratures common in the rest of the state. The Panhandle itself reaches some five hundred miles, from the Canadian border on the east up to Icy Bay on the Gulf of Alaska. Within this area is the Alexander Archipelago, a maze of a thousand islands, and a coastal strip cleft with Norwegian-like fiords and the snow-covered coastal range.

Half the world's glaciers exist in the Gulf Coast, which ex-tends for 650 miles to form a great arc. There are many glaciers in the Alaska Range, but the huge, grinding masses of ice that move toward the ocean calve icebergs that drift down into the northern Pacific. The largest glacier, Malaspina, is bigger than the entire state of Rhode Island, and mountains rise to 19,000 feet. The region also includes Kodiak Island, Prince William Sound, and Cook Inlet. Cook Inlet has an amazing tidal varia-tion of 34 feet. Located on the inlet is Alaska's largest city, Anchorage, which contains about half the state's population.

The worst weather in the world characterizes the Alaska Pen-insula and the Aleutian Islands. The last island of the Aleutian chain, which extends for eleven hundred miles, is actually the southernmost point in Alaska. The rain, fog, and gale-force winds have kept the population down to a few whites, three thousand Aleuts, and five thousand military personnel.

Ranging north brings one to the Eskimos, most of whom—some sixteen thousand—live in western Alaska. Access to the region is limited to summer because of the ice on the Bering Sea, which is encountered to the north of the rich fishing ground of Bristol Bay and extends into the Arctic Ocean. The twenty-three-hundred-mile Yukon River and, below it, the Kuskowim River, form deltas on the Bering Sea.

Northern Alaska is as cold as its name implies. Air temperatures are not so low as those in the interior, but the wind-chill factor produces the equivalent of temperatures of minus one hundred degrees. Most of the Arctic region north of the Brooks Range is low and filled with lakes and marshes. Inland, caribou range the tundra, which in the summer brightens with flowers and herbs. Summer ice pack conditions are unpredictable. In 1975, the barge fleet carrying equipment from Seattle to Prudhoe had great trouble navigating, and some of the ships turned back.

The interior of Alaska lies between two mountain ranges—the Brooks on the north and the Alaska on the south—and is cut by the Yukon River. Despite the fact that winter temperatures reach sixty below (wind chill aside), the wind does not blow much; and Fairbanks, Alaska's second largest city, has a bearable climate. White spruce, aspen, paper birch, and poplar forests cover the interior region.

The famous North Slope petroleum development in the northeastern corner of Alaska is only one in a series of "discoveries" of wealth in Alaska, following earlier hopes for great fortunes from gold, salmon, and furs. That oil reserves exist on the north side of the Brooks Range actually has been known for more than a century: an explorer of the Hudson's Bay Company, Thomas Simpson, observed oil deposits along the Arctic Shore during a coastal survey from 1836 to 1839.

Alaska remains the land of potential. It may not be coincidental that Jonathan Swift located his land of the giants in the North Pacific. Alaska is truly a land of Brobdingnagian proportions.

And yet Lilliput may be, for Alaska, a more appropriate metaphor from *Gulliver's Travels:* time and again, Alaskans have felt themselves hampered by the invisible strings that reach to the economic and political forces of the United States, particularly to Washington, D.C. Sandy Smith and others were not able to make their fortunes in Alaska because of these external restraints. And so it has been with the timbermen of the southeast, the salmon fishermen of the North Pacific and the Bering Sea, the merchants, professional men, and housewives of the towns and villages. All these thought of themselves as untrammeled individuals, free from the restrictions and pressures of the more populous parts of the world. Yet in the end, larger, impersonal forces have been more determinative.

2

From Native Alaska to Russian America

*T*HE discoverers of America were also the continent's first human occupants—restless hunters who followed their game across the tundra that connected northwestern America with northeastern Siberia. They became the ancestors of all of America's aboriginal peoples. Our knowledge of these Asiatics is vague, but they apparently made their trek over the land bridge sometime between ten thousand and forty thousand years ago. Subsequently, the waters of the Bering Sea submerged the passageway, to sever the two continents. Descendants of these early hunters include the three broad, general groups of native Alaskans: Aleuts, Eskimos, and Indians.

Ages passed before Europeans rediscovered Alaska, although Siberian and American natives had long since been crossing the narrow Bering Strait to trade. The initial Russian contact with Alaska's natives in the eighteenth century was with the Aleuts. The Aleuts, like all other North American aboriginals, descended from the Siberians who migrated from Asia over the Bering Sea land bridge. These people settled on the Alaskan mainland for a time before moving out to the Aleutian Islands, probably about three thousand years ago. The movement did not reflect any inherited longing to move nearer to the origin place

11

of their ancestors; rather, the food resources of the island chain attracted the Aleuts.

Aleut villages were usually located on the shores of the northern side of the islands because the Bering Sea sustained more sea mammal and fish life than the North Pacific Ocean did. Also, the coast of the Bering Sea offered better opportunities to gather driftwood on the beaches and to find whales that had stranded themselves on shore. Villages consisted of a number of dwellings dug into the ground and roofed with driftwood, earth, and grass.

Aleut women and children gathered food available on the island—a variety of berries, edible greens, and herbs that were used for medicinal purposes. Foxes and other small animals were trapped, but there were no large land animals. Of necessity, the Aleuts had to become masters of maritime hunting, and in this activity they had no equals among North American natives. Most of the Aleuts' sustenance came from the sea. They fished and hunted sea mammals steadily. The Aleut adapted most successfully to his marine environment. Boatsmen used spears and harpoons to kill seals, sea otters, sea lions, walrus, and sea cows. Dexterity and coolness were essential attributes of a hunter bobbing on a lively sea with just seconds to take aim and throw his weapon before his prey could dive beneath the surface of the water.

As skilled boatsmen, the Aleuts could propel their slender, skin-covered kayaks through waters often stormy in winter and foggy in summer. The turbulence of the Bering Sea is the result of the meeting of the Pacific Ocean with the cooler waters of the Bering Sea. To meet that harsh climate the people developed into excellent and inventive craftsmen. They were, in addition, accomplished artists. The kayak showed keen appreciation of the design dictum that form follows function. The kayak was light in weight and could be carried easily by one man. The boatsman could dart after his prey at great speed, propelling the boat with a double-bladed paddle. And, most important, the boat could be made absolutely water-tight. Aleut artistry in decorative arts was expressed in ornamenting the kayak's bow and paddles and other objects. They made wooden hats decorated with sea-lion bristles, colored stones, and feathers. They also made and decorated amulets, charms, masks, baskets, parkas, and festive dance costumes.

The people respected leading warriors but did not recognize chiefs except when making war. Their loose social system was centered on the family, and they had no system of keeping order or punishing misdeeds beyond the vengeance extracted by a victim's kin. It was considered a firm duty for a family to use violent means to avenge grievances against family members.

Aleuts married when they reached the age of puberty. Men were entitled to as many wives as they could maintain and were free to send women back to their families at any time. Keeping of concubines, male and female, was also permissible. A man sometimes allowed a visitor to sleep with his wife, not as a matter of prostitution, but as part of a complicated social pattern by which special relationships were maintained.

Unlike many other aboriginals, the Aleuts did not abandon dwellings after a member's death. Also they mummified some of the distinguished dead. Mummies were laid in kayaks, placed in dry caves, and surrounded with objects they had cherished in life. Sometimes the people held wakes for as long as forty days. Both husbands and wives were expected to pull out their hair, rend their garments, and otherwise express their grief on the death of a mate. Slaves, usually foes captured on a raid, were sometimes killed when their master died.

The Aleutian Island environment differs markedly from that of other regions of Alaska in climate and physical geography. Rainfall is heavy, and violent winds—the williwaws—sweep over the unforested islands. But the islands are just a little north of Seattle in latitude and do not have severely cold winters. It is unusual for the winter temperature to fall below 25 degrees Fahrenheit.

Eskimos inhabited Kodiak Island when the Russian fur traders moved into Alaska. This large mountainous island lies near the mouth of Cook Inlet. Kodiak's people suffered at Russian hands as did the Aleuts, being compelled to hunt and work for the traders, whom they served at the expense of their own livelihood.

In the popular mind, the Eskimo is associated with the Arctic Coast, where he dwells in a snow house and subsists on whale meat. In actuality, only a small portion of Alaskan Eskimos live in the Arctic today, and that was also true at the time of the first European contact when two thirds of the total Eskimo-Aleut population lived on islands or along the coast of the Bering Sea. There are three major Eskimo groups: the Pacific Eskimos; the Bering Sea Eskimos, or Yupik; and the Arctic Eskimos, or Inuit. Each group has its particular characteristics.

When eighteenth-century Siberians crossed the Bering Sea to hunt for furs, there were approximately 8,700 Yupik-speaking Pacific Eskimos living on Kodiak Island, the Alaska Peninsula, and along Prince William Sound. These people hunted marine mammals and birds and took salmon from the streams. Despite the abundance of sea mammals and fish, periodic famines occurred when game patterns varied. Kodiak Island had the highest density of population, while the people living along Prince William Sound were widely scattered.

The Bering Sea Eskimos numbered about nine thousand and depended primarily upon the resources of the sea and rivers. They also hunted caribou where the animals ranged. Bering Sea Eskimos had the greatest population and formed the oldest culture of all Eskimo tribes.

In the Arctic, there were only 6,350 Inuits at contact by whites in the eighteenth century. Population density was low— two persons per one hundred square kilometers—because of the comparative scarcity of food resources. These Eskimos distinguished themselves in their ability to hunt whales from their large skin boats. Eskimo hunters from the coast ventured into the interior on hunting parties on occasion and some families established permanent inland villages.

Traditional Eskimo customs and social organizations varied widely from place to place even within the same major groups. Marriages were usually monogamous, but polygamy was customary in several villages. With a few exceptions, most notably with shamans—the Alaskan natives' equivalent of the medicine man—people were expected to be unobtrusive members of the community. Eskimos believed that shamans possessed extrasensory powers enabling them to cure the ailing, determine the weather, and forecast the future. Those who convinced villagers of their supernatural power had great influence. A shaman could, however, fall from favor if others came to suspect that he was using his demonic powers to cause harm.

Eskimo villages typically consisted of about two hundred persons, two families housed in each of the ten to fifteen dwellings. Individuals held obligations to family, sharers of the dwelling, and to relatives. Inhabitants owed no allegiance to the village at large, however, in contrast to the Aleuts. Eskimos did maintain community centers called *karigis* or *kazigi,* depending on the region. Men and boys socialized in these large houses and sometimes slept and ate there. They also played games and prepared hunting equipment in them.

Most Eskimos explained their origin as the work of Raven. The fabled bird, personified as a god, also created beings of the land and sea and was credited with having distributed the Eskimo population. The Eskimos told traditional tales, varying from place to place, that explained the sun and the moon. Strangely enough, the moon was more important in mythology than the sun. It was also believed that shamans often voyaged to the moon to gain supernatural help.

The natives liked charms representing different animals or parts of the animal itself as a favored means of getting along with spirits. Belief in the power of spirits to help or hinder individuals formed the core of the Eskimos' religious convictions. Even lakes and mountains had spirits who had to be respected on the proper occasions. The people invoked these higher powers in song before beginning a hunting journey or other significant event.

Eskimos traded with their neighbors, sometimes feuded with them, and made raids, but they also held community social exchanges. One such, the Messenger Feast, was launched by sending messengers from one village to another bearing a communitywide invitation. The messengers carried sticks telling in symbolic form what gifts the hosts would like to receive. An exchange of gifts was the point of the event, although there was much feasting, game-playing, and dancing, as well.

Feasts also celebrated the memory of the dead. Minor feasts might be held three or four times a year, and a Great Feast of the Dead was conducted in some places at intervals of four to ten years. On such occasions, the souls of the deceased were freed from the earth forever. In the name of the dead, relatives distributed food and gifts at such gatherings.

The Eskimo culture, with whaling as the chief hunting activity, showed a high degree of social organization. Bering Sea and Arctic Ocean villagers organized into boat crews, usually made up of six men. For crew leaders the villagers chose only men who were highly respected for their hunting abilities. Before the hunting season, village folk performed a number of rituals designed to propitiate the spirit of the whale. Once the sea ice opened, a constant watch was maintained. Hunters launched their boats whenever bowhead or white whales appeared and rowed out to engage the prey. A strong arm would hurl the harpoon at the giant mammal, and when the weapon equipped with line stuck fast, the crewmen towed the whale back to the beach for butchering and distribution.

Alaskan Indians included the Tlingits, of southeastern Alaska; the Haidas, of Prince of Wales Island; the Tsimshian, of Annette Island; and the widely distributed Athabascans, consisting of twelve distinct groups: the Koyukon, Kutchin, Han, Tanacross, Tanana, Upper Tanana, Ahtna, Tanaina, Upper Kuskokwim, Holikachuk, Ingalik, and Eyak.

Athabascans (sometimes called Athapaskans) were spread over a wide region at first contact with whites. In the nineteenth century, there were thirty-five hundred Athabascan Indians in the Yukon-Kuskokwin basins, some seven hundred in the Cook Inlet-Susitna River basin, between three hundred and four hundred in the Copper River basin, and about five thousand in the Arctic Drainage Lowlands, most of which is within Canada. These Indians hunted land animals (and sea mammals as well, in the case of the Cook Inlet Tanaina Indians), fished, and trapped in a land not prolific in animal resources and subject to severe winter climates. To survive, Athabascans had to acquire a high degree of flexibility.

Beyond the immediate family, Indians formed only a loose

social organization. They borrowed the potlatch custom from southeastern Alaskan Indians—the Tlingits—but did not observe it in the same manner. Superficially, the potlatch was a feast honoring one who has died. It was carried on like an Irish wake with dancing and feasting, and it culminated in the distribution of gifts. But for the Athabascans, greater importance lay in the prestige gained by the party-giver. To gain and hold public esteem, one had to celebrate the death of even distant relatives lavishly.

Animal and other spirits were critical forces in the beliefs of Athabascans. They feared some spirits and respected others, such as the animals they depended upon for sustenance. Indian hunters placated all spirits with a number of rituals, songs, taboos, charms, and amulets. Success on the hunt was essential to life, and hunters assiduously courted animal spirits. They knew how to treat slain animals carefully, butcher them according to form, and display them in a way particular to each species.

Athabascan Indians hunted caribou, moose, and bear with bow and arrow. They also took caribou and fur-bearing animals with snares, and bear in deadfalls. Fish provided an important source of food for people of the Yukon Valley and Cook Inlet, but dependence on fish varied widely. If game was scarce and if the local rivers were not so swift or muddy, Athabascans caught salmon and dried it for winter use. Winter subsistence posed a particular problem. The Indians developed snowshoes that allowed them to stalk game over the snow, and in some regions they fished through the ice. But the necessity of ranging widely for food in the winter curtailed community life for many Indians. They scattered in family groups in pursuit of game, and they certainly knew periods of starvation.

Anthropologists and ethnohistorians have had difficulty in defining the nature of Athabascan social institutions and religious beliefs as practiced before any contact with whites. From mid-nineteenth century onward, missionaries influenced most groups and altered the aboriginal patterns of life and thought. It has been observed, however, that the natives accepted Christianity from the beginning as a complementary system that did

not conflict with their basic attitudes and beliefs. The Athabascans' perception of the supernatural world was general enough
to be accommodating. Yet whenever primary matters such as
food gathering, health, and forecasting the future concerned the
Indians, they relied upon traditional beliefs.

Any one of numerous Athabascan legends conveys the
wonder and respect in which the people perceived supernatural
beings. *Denali* was the name Indians called North America's
highest peak, Mount McKinley, and they told a story of its origin that is rich in eroticism, powerful magic, and cunning. The
legend even includes explanations of game management: snow
and glaciers on the mountain were designed to keep the sheep
from escaping the wolves; geese were allowed to smash into the
mountain so that their flesh could provide carrion for the raven.
Everything had its place and purpose in the well-ordered
legends of the Athabascan Indians, as with all other Alaskan native cultures.

The Tlingits of southeastern Alaska numbered around about
ten thousand at the time of Russian contact in the 1700s. There
were about eight thousand Haidas who inhabited the south end
of Prince of Wales Island, but it is uncertain when they migrated from Canada. The Tsimshian Indians of Annette Island
did not move there from Canada until 1887. Indians of the
Northwest Coast shared a common culture from Yakutat Bay to
northern California, and it was a richly diversified one. They
enjoyed a moderate climate, because of the influence of the Japanese current; and an abundant food supply aided the development of a complex or "high" culture—the highest, in fact, of
any American aboriginals north of Mexico. The sea and the
rivers provided salmon, cod, herring, candlefish, mollusks,
seal, sea otter, sea lion, porpoise, and whale. To supplement
marine sources of food, such game animals as deer, bear, wolf,
mink, and martens were plentiful. When a people can gather
food easily, they have time to express their energies in other
ways. The seasonal nature of the salmon harvest suggested and
encouraged the idea of leisure. Once the Northwest Coast Indians had caught all the fish they needed and had preserved

enough to keep them until the next year's run, there was little provisioning work to do.

Having access to abundant stands of western hemlock, Sitka spruce, and western red cedar, and farther south, Alaska cedar, all the native groups of Alaska's Northwest Coast specialized in wood carpentry to produce excellently finished and highly decorated products of all kinds: canoes, totem poles, house facings and entrances, boxes, dishes, and cooking utensils. They also used wood to build their houses—large, rectangular, gable-roofed, neatly joined structures. Other Alaskan natives lived in primitive dwellings by comparison; the Aleuts, Athabascans, and Eskimos lacked materials, and above all, they also lacked the leisure of the southeastern Alaskans. Canoes built by the Northwest Coast Indians varied in size. Many had a high, projecting bow and stern that withstood sea waves effectively. Because of the rugged, mountainous terrain along most of the coast, the Indians traveled almost exclusively at sea in these canoes. The Haidas of the Queen Charlotte Islands produced the most prized craft. Made of specially selected, clear-grained red cedar, these canoes were as long as fifty feet and seven to eight feet wide. Boatsmen propelled their canoes with paddles.

It was usually the Indian women who wove intricate baskets and enhanced their appearance with interesting and colorful designs. One of the most valued trade items was the skillfully woven Chilkat blanket. These beautiful articles, woven from mountain-goat wool and dyed, were objects of pride to their owners, who displayed them at special feasts and often were wrapped in them at death. The Indians manufactured garments of wood and of cedar bark, making both everyday wear and more exotic clothing for dances and festive occasions. All Indian craftsmanship expressed inventiveness, a strong sense of color and form, great skill, and, of course, the wealth of a region that supplied plenty of diverse materials.

As might be expected, the diversity of Indian society was also strongly expressed in social organization. No other Alaskan aboriginal culture compared in complexity to that of the southeastern Alaskan tribes. They maintained a system of hereditary rank and chieftainship and matrilineal descent. Strict rules governed a choice of marital partners. Among the Tlingits there were two major divisions, Wolf and Raven. A Wolf man had to take his wife from the Raven division, and any children born would also become part of the Raven division.

The Indians further divided into clans, a clan being a social unit with its own dwellings, berry grounds, fishing areas, and government by its own chiefs. Typically, a clan would be composed of a group of brothers, their sisters' sons, sons of the sisters of the second generation, and maternal cousins. The men's own sons would belong to the lineages of their mothers according to the rules of the matrilineal system. These clans sometimes acted in common with others—in making war, for instance—but only by entering a formal alliance.

The potlatch was the most important ceremony of these Indians. Before an individual could assume his right to use properties held in common by the clan, he had to announce his claim at a potlatch. The claimant insured the good will of his invited guests by offering a feast and lavishing gifts upon them. Normally tribal chiefs presented the potlatch on behalf of a family member's claims, consequently the ceremony was an important element in group solidarity. It expressed the closeness of the family and the acknowledgement of the chief's leadership.

Festivities of the Tlingits and other tribes showed variations on the basic purpose of the potlatch. Tlingits saw it also as a ritual, sometimes of several years' duration, for mourning the death of a chief. The potlatch feast rewarded the people who conducted funeral rites for the chief. On that occasion the clan also solicited craftsmen to carve a mortuary column or to build a house for the new chief. Beyond serving practical matters, these functions bound the members more closely into their social unit.

Alaskan Indians believed that there was a supreme being or beings, and they believed in the immortality of animal species essential to the people. They performed certain rituals to make sure that such animals did not fail to come their way. As with all Indians, the Alaskans practiced such rituals as a normal part in daily life while preparing for the fishing season, a hunting or war party, births, marriages, deaths, and other occasions. They had no systematized beliefs about their origin or about the cosmos and no formal arrangement of supernatural beings. Indians did, however, express their diversity in supernatural matters through a rich oral literature of myths and legends that were particular to certain regions.

The cultural clash that occurred between Alaskan natives and the Europeans moving into Alaska did not differ markedly from that of other North American frontiers. It produced a drastic impact that resulted in violence and oppression initially and in belated efforts to protect and to educate the natives. No clear record exists of a European ship's reaching the high latitudes of the North Pacific until the eighteenth century. Russians came to Alaska as part of a concerted effort to evaluate and develop the resources of their eastern provinces. In 1724 Peter the Great decreed that Siberia and neighboring regions must be explored. At the time, Peter did not even know whether Asia and North America were separated. By the late seventeenth century, cossacks had ventured into Siberia as far as the Pacific Ocean in quest of furs, but there still remained much doubt of northern geography.

Peter selected Vitus Bering, a Dane in Russian service, to head the exploring expedition. Bering's task was not light. Siberia spans five thousand miles from the Ural Mountains to the Pacific Ocean. An army of men, including ship builders and crew, as well as expedition equipment and provisions had to be transported over great distances to Okhotsk.

Bering labored for more than three years, transporting supplies and building ships. It was the summer of 1728 before the *St. Gabriel* was launched and Bering could sail north to fulfill the first part of his instructions. He passed through—and named—the Bering Strait and convinced himself that the continents were not joined at any point further north. The explorers also landed upon and named St. Lawrence Island in the Bering Strait. The expedition marked the first time for Europeans to set foot on any part of Alaska, but the fog throughout the Bering Strait voyage prevented them from glimpsing the North American mainland.

Bering returned to St. Petersburg and made his report. He

recommended exploration of North America and the establishment of a sea route from Kamchatka to Japan. Both ventures
could result in the development of trade. Bering also urged further exploration of Siberia. The imperial government approved
these recommendations in 1733 and placed Bering in command
of a new expedition. The second venture was to be more ambitious than Bering's first expedition. Authorities even assigned
scientists to assess the resources of Siberia and of any newly
discovered lands.

In the summer of 1741, Bering launched the *St. Peter* and the
St. Paul at Okhotsk and sailed the vessels to Avacha Bay on the
east coast of Kamchatka to make final preparations for the
American voyage. Unfortunately, the Russian senate had issued
ambiguous sailing orders to Bering, suggesting that he search
for land southeast of Kamchatka.

Map makers of that day customarily showed a large land
mass in the North Pacific, called Jeso or Gama Land. Bering
and his officers considered sailing directly to the east, where the
American continent had been reported, but they were influenced
by the government's wishes to direct their courses for Jeso. The
naval officers made a tragic error in seeking an imaginary land.
Once their ships passed over the waters where land was supposed to be, Bering altered their course to the east. But valuable
time had been lost, and the odds rose steeply against a safe return.

Bering could not maintain contact with the *St. Paul*, commanded by Alexei Chirikov, because of fog and foul weather.
The two captains maintained similar courses, however, and both
made landfalls in southeastern Alaska in mid-July. Chirikov lost
two boats and fifteen men who either drowned or were killed by
Indians, but he did manage a successful return five months after
sailing from Kamchatka.

Scurvy ravaged the crews of both ships. Because of that sick-
ness, Bering resolved to return to Kamchatka after his initial
landfall. His decision pained the expedition's German scientist,
Georg Wilhelm Steller, who recognized the opportunities
opened to the first scientist to study the natural wonders of
Northwestern America. Steller urged Bering to winter over in

Alaska but Bering, sick and aging, would not consider it. He reasoned that he had fulfilled his mission. Others could follow up on his discovery. Bering sent a watering party ashore on Kayak Island, off the Gulf of Alaska coast, and reluctantly allowed Steller to scamper around for a few hours gathering specimens of flora and fauna. "I could not help saying," remarked Steller bitterly, "that we had come only for the purpose of bringing American water to Asia." [1]

Bering's *St. Peter* made slow progress on the return voyage. Gales buffeted the ship almost continuously for weeks. Bering navigated along the Aleutian Chain until forced to run the battered ship ashore on the island off Kamchatka that bears his name. Bering and many seamen died of scurvy over the winter; the survivors built another ship and reached Kamchatka the following summer.

Because of the ship's grounding, Steller gained the time he had longed for to investigate new lands. He classified novel plants and described the features of seals, sea otters, birds, foxes, and other animals. He also dissected and described the giant manatee, or Steller's sea cow, which was to be hunted to extinction by the Russians a few years later.

Steller recorded the first meeting between Russians and Aleuts before the *St. Peter* was wrecked. He praised the natives' appearance and handicrafts. The fleeting encounter followed the pattern of European-aboriginal contact. Initially all parties expressed friendliness, until a misunderstanding or supposed aggression occurred. The Russians fired their muskets over the heads of the natives and laughed as the startled islanders dived to the ground. Steller noted that the Aleuts "waved their hands to us to be off quickly as they did not want us any longer." [2]

The Aleuts may have wished the Russians away, but it was to no avail; for Steller and the other survivors of Bering's crew had carried a number of sea-otter pelts back to Kamchatka. Sea otters produced a five-foot-long pelt of brown-black, glossy fur that was highly valued in the Chinese market. Siberian fur

1. F. A. Golder, *Bering's Voyages,* 2 vols. (New York: American Graphic Society, 1922), 2:37.
2. Golder, *Bering's Voyages,* 2:95.

traders lost little time in preparing to reap the fur harvest of the Aleutian and Commander islands. The new lands promised wealth to those who dared to navigate the stormy waters of the Bering Sea.

The sea otter's valuable fur opened the Alaskan frontier to commercial exploitation and led to the first European settlements. That development paralleled the westward movement in other parts of North America where the beaver drew Americans and Canadians toward the Pacific.

Russian traders made thirty-three voyages into the Bering Sea in the twenty years following the return of Bering's men. They were unskilled as shipbuilders and navigators but could recognize the boating and hunting talents of the Aleuts. As a matter of course, the traders enslaved the Aleuts, forcing the men to hunt sea otter by holding their wives and children as hostages.

Shipowners who financed fur-trading voyages expected traders to return with enough furs to yield a one hundred percent profit on costs of building and provisioning a ship. Traders competed fiercely with each other for control of new hunting grounds, and violence sometimes erupted. In the later years of the eighteen century, British and American traders rivaled the Russians as well. After James Cook's third expedition for England from 1776 to 1780, revealed the abundance of sea otters along the entire coast from California to the Aleutians, venturesome traders sailed from old and New England to gather furs.

Russian traders customarily remained on their hunting voyages in the Aleutians for two to five years, but Gregory Shelikhov, whose fur-trading company became the nucleus of the later Russian American Company, changed that pattern. In 1784 Shelikhov established a permanent base on Kodiak Island, after a furious battle with the Eskimos who lived there. Shelikhov had professed his kind intentions on first encountering the natives; yet, understandably enough, they were hostile, knowing full well that the Aleuts had been enslaved. The Eskimos attempted an ambush, but Shelikhov had anticipated it: ''The savages came down from their rocks in great numbers, and fell upon us with such fury, that I verily believe they would have effected their purpose without difficulty, had we been less vigilant, or more timid." In this and subsequent encounters, the arrows of the Eskimos were no match for European muskets. Shelikhov stressed the courage of the Russians in his narrative: "The prospect of death inspired us with courage; we defended ourselves with our firearms; and, though not till after an obstinate engagement, put them to flight." [3]

With Kodiak as a base, Shelikhov was in a good position to compete with other Russian traders. He dispatched Aleut hunters to Cook Inlet and Prince William Sound, which were just to the north and east of the island, or sent them to seek otters in the Aleutian Islands' waters to the northwest. The base also gave Shelikhov a better bargaining position with the Russian government. For years he had tried to convince the czar's officials that the rivalry of fur traders was wasteful and detrimental to Russian and Aleut peoples. He promised profits, stability, and the expansion of Christianity to Alaska if his company were granted a monopoly of the fur trade. In 1799 the czar did grant an exclusive charter to Shelikhov's Russian-American Company. By that time, Shelikhov was dead, and Nikolai Rezanov headed the company, with Alexander Baranov as chief manager of the colonies.

Rezanov and Baranov pursued the policies formulated by Shelikhov. The nature of the Russian enterprise demanded expansion. Once the otter of one area were depleted, new hunting grounds had to be exploited. Shelikhov had expressed that basic need more grandly: "For rapidly extending the power of the Russian people it is possible to step farther and farther along the shore on the American continent, at the furthest extension to California." [4]

Baranov founded a station in southeastern Alaska at Sitka in 1799 and became virtually the governor of all Russian activities in North America. The natives of the region were Tlingit Indians who were restive at the Russian presence even though no

3. Melvin B. Ricks, *The Earliest History of Alaska* (Anchorage: Cook Inlet Historical Society, 1970), p. 5.

4. C. L. Andrews, "Russian Plans for American Domination," *Washington Historical Quarterly*, April 1927, p. 84.

attempt was made to enslave the Indians as had been done with the Aleuts. By this time, English and American ships traded along the northwest coast, and the Indians were eagerly acquiring firearms. In 1802 the Tlingits attacked the Russian fort at Sitka and won a bloody victory. The fort was burned and 408 of the 450 defenders were killed. Later, the Indians killed 200 Aleut hunters as well.

Baranov revenged himself on the Tlingits in 1804. A Russian frigate called at Kodiak, and Baranov persuaded its commander to join an attack on Sitka. The Tlingits repelled the initial attack of Russians and Aleuts, killing ten and wounding twenty-six, including Baranov. Baranov then withdrew his force until the frigate bombarded the Indians' fortified position. The frigate's guns forced an evacuation of the fort. To expedite their flight, the warriors killed all the children of the village.

During that time, Rezanov unsuccessfully attempted to open trade with Japan. In 1805 he inspected the Russian colonies and reported on his ambitions to the czar. He decided to make Sitka (New Archangel) the colonial capital and to establish bases on Vancouver Island, the Columbia River, and in California. He intended to drive the American mariners from the fur trade by force. American ships from New England had gained most of the furs from the coast south of Alaska and competed directly with the Russians by selling them at Canton, China. Rezanov pointed out that Spanish claims to the Northwest Coast could be ignored because Spain was not strong enough to enforce them. The Spanish had ventured into Alaskan waters some years earlier to investigate the Russian intrusion, but these voyages were the last gasp of a dying empire.

Rezanov can be credited with being Alaska's first conservationist. He was aware that the Steller's sea cow had already become extinct because it was hunted so relentlessly for food by fur traders, and he knew that otters were becoming more difficult to find. After inspecting the fur-seal rookeries of the Pribilof Islands and learning that more than a million seals had been taken for their fur, he banned any further butchering in order to prevent their total extermination. Fur-seal pelts did not command the high prices on the Chinese market that those of sea otters did; yet Rezanov recognized the wisdom of managing the resource for future needs.

Rezanov's inspection also revealed that harsh treatment of the Aleuts had not ceased with the grant of a monopoly to the Russian American Company. A companion of Rezanov's commented upon the "oppression under which they labor." The Aleuts did not even own their own boats and clothes—everything was considered company property. "The stewards and overseers order as many people of either sex as they have occasion for, to go out hunting, or compel them to do other kinds of work as they please, to prepare skins, to make clothes, to fabricate baidarkas [two-man canoes]; to clean and dry fish." The situation of Russian sailors and laborers was not much better. "They are extremely ill-treated," reported Rezanov's naturalist and physician, G. H. von Langsdorff, "and kept at their work till their strength is entirely exhausted." Workers received no medical treatment, and their food and housing were wretched. After years of work, the Russians often found themselves owing the company money for clothes and other necessities. "They then strive to drown their cares in brandy and should they be strong enough to survive so many trials, must esteem themselves fortunate, if, after many years spent in hardships and privations, they return home at last with empty pockets, ruined constitutions, and minds wholly depressed and broken down." [5]

The company acquired exclusive trade rights under a Russian charter that was renewed in 1821 and again in 1844. The company was effectively the only government in the Alaskan colonies, wielding political, economic, and military control over its vast monopoly. There were no courts in the colonies, but the charter provided that in serious cases the accused be sent to the nearest Russian authorities at Okhotsk, Siberia, while lesser matters were to be dealt with by the governor or referred to a special commission. The governor maintained complete authority over the people, whether Russian, Creole (mixed European and native blood), or native. Russian employees contracted to

5. Georg H. Langsdorff, *Voyages and Travels in Various Parts of the World,* 2 vols. (Amsterdam: Israel, 1968), 2:71.

work for the company for a seven-year term, yet the term could be renewed for another seven years merely upon the request of the company. Those owing money to the company could be held until their debts were paid. Employees were "subjects" as long as the governor was the representative of the czar, with unchallenged economic and political control over them.

Natives had the theoretical right under the charter of complaining to the Governing Board in St. Petersburg against abuse of local authorities. Needless to say, the right of appeal from such distance by those whose petition could only pass through company channels was an illusory one. Native chieftains became company subordinates and helped to maintain political and social control over the natives for the benefit of the traders.

Russian and Creole employees did not even have the natives' right of appeal to the company governing board. Presumably it was felt that government authorities in Siberia could look after their rights, yet it was illegal to transmit complaints by a third person. That left a complainant in the awkward position of needing permission to secure passage on a company ship in order to appeal to governmental authorities.

It could be argued that the company was never more than formally a private enterprise, but was comparable to an independent governmental department. Even the original 1799 charter required the company management to report directly to the czar everything relating to the affairs of the company, and, as time went on, governmental control was further extended by appointment of naval officers in the colonial administration and by establishment of a permanent council for the company, consisting primarily of government officials selected by the government.

In 1812, at the direction of Alexander Baranov, the Russians built a post in California, Fort Ross, just north of San Francisco. Ross was manned by 26 Russians and 102 Aleuts. The Russians raised crops and animals, and the Aleuts hunted sea otter along the California coast. Baranov's plans were not fulfilled as successfully as had been anticipated. He had hoped that the food produced at Fort Ross would suffice to sustain the colonies in Alaska, but poor soil and primitive farming methods resulted in a mediocre output. The company maintained the post for thirty years, despite the protests of the Spanish and, later, the Mexicans, before selling it to John Sutter, an American.

Baranov made one other short-lived attempt to solve the provisioning problem and further Russian hegemony over the North Pacific. He sent an agent to Hawaii to try to establish beneficial relations. The agent blundered into supporting the losing side in a clash between native factions and had to run for his life. Baranov then disavowed him and gave up his plans for Hawaii.

After Baranov retired in 1818, Russian naval officers managed the colonies. A former explorer, Baron Ferdinand von Wrangel, who was manager from 1830 to 1835, was the most brilliant of these. Wrangel founded a fort near the mouth of the Yukon in 1833, in order to tap the Yukon River trade, and checkmated the ambitious rivalry of the English Hudson's Bay Company traders by blocking the entry to the Stikine River with another fort.

Wrangel sought further to solve the food provisioning problem. More land in California—then under Mexican control—would have to be acquired to improve production. Wrangel proposed to ask the new revolutionary government of Mexico to approve an enlargement of Fort Ross. After finishing his term as governor, Wrangel journeyed to Mexico City and negotiated with President Santa Anna, who was then deeply concerned with the Texas uprising. Wrangel put forward some good arguments. A settlement of a few Russians presented no threat and might deter the encroachments of English and Americans on California soil. Santa Anna lent an ear to the scheme but insisted that Russia recognize his new nation. Wrangel pleaded with the czar for this *quid pro quo* when he returned to St. Petersburg, but to no avail. The czar was interested in crushing revolutions rather than honoring them with recognition. Wrangel was convinced that except for that stubbornness Russia might have succeeded in dominating all of California and in provisioning the Alaskan colonies. Had that occurred, it is likely that there would have been less sentiment for the sale of the colonies to the United States in 1867.

Yet other factors influenced events. The Russians pursued the development of the Amur valley of Siberia, which held a large population and valuable natural resources. The population of Russian America varied between five hundred and eight hundred over the years, and its fur resources were dwindling. Neither economic nor strategic purposes seemed important enough to the Russians to hold distant colonies that could be lost to England or the United States in a time of war. St. Petersburg apparently also resented some of the company's policies. When Baron Edoard de Stoeckl, the Russian minister to the United States, reported his opinion favoring a sale of the region in the 1860s, he commented on the neglect of the company: "The status of the Indians on the islands under our rule had not been improved either physically or morally, and the tribes on the mainland continued to be as savage and hostile as they were at the time of the discovery." The population remained too small, and "no effort has been made as yet to explore the interior of the country and to try to benefit by the resources it could offer." [6]

The Russian government also recognized that it could not protect the North Pacific and Arctic Ocean resources that it claimed as its own. American whalers entered the Kodiak ground, south of the Aleutians, in 1835. Ten years later, the hunters moved into the Bering Sea in pursuit of the bowhead whale; and in 1848, the first Yankee ship hunted the Arctic waters of Alaska. Thousands of whales and walrus were taken, and most shipowners profited enormously. The Russian American Company asked the Russian government to provide a naval force, but in vain.

In 1821, Czar Alexander II had responded to a complaint about the intrusion of American trading vessels in Alaskan waters by issuing a *ukase* banning "the transaction of commerce, and the pursuit of whaling and fishing, or any other industry . . . all along the North West Coast of America from the Bering Sea to the 51st parallel." [7] The *ukase* further prohibited any foreign vessel's putting ashore or approaching within one

6. Ernest Gruening, editor, *An Alaskan Reader: 1867–1967* (New York: Meredith Press, 1966), p. 43.

7. John J. Underwood, *Alaska: An Empire in the Making* (New York: Dodd, Mead, 1913), p. 265.

hundred miles of the coast. Britain and the United States protested the *ukase,* and Alexander retreated. Conventions of 1824 and 1825 gave ships the right to call at Russian ports with the approval of local authorities.

In the 1820s, Russia was powerless to resist the intrusions of the Americans and even more impotent to do so in the 1850s and 1860s, after the Crimean War defeat had weakened the government.

Thus, for a number of reasons, Russia agreed to sell its northern territory to the United States. In 1867, Minister Baron Edoard de Stoeckl and Secretary of State William Henry Seward drew up a treaty of cession in Washington that set a price of $7.2 million.

3

Colonial Rule

$\mathcal{O}$N April 19, 1867, the United States Senate consented to
the treaty of cession that had been signed by Secretary of State
Seward and Stoeckl, Russian Minister to Washington. President
Andrew Johnson signed the document on May 28, and a month
later the treaty was proclaimed. Among those who supported the
treaty's ratification in the Senate was Charles Sumner of Massachusetts, who made a convincing, knowledgeable address.
Sumner reviewed the wonders and potential wealth of Alaska in
terms that left no doubt of the wisdom of the acquisition. He
summoned up images of "forests of pine and fir waiting for the
axe; then the mineral products, among which are coal and copper, if not iron, silver, lead, and gold." Then the senator from
Massachusetts lightened the burden of his testimony with a little
humor. Alaska also held "the two great products of New England, granite and ice." But most important were the fur-
bearing animals and the fisheries—"fisheries which, in waters
superabundant with animal life beyond any of the globe, seem
to promise a new commerce." Sumner assured his auditors that
he had not been engaging in hyperbole in singing praises of
Alaska. He had cited authorities for his remarks. "I have done
little more than hold the scales. If these incline on either side, it
is because reason or testimony on that side is the weightier." In
conclusion, Senator Sumner asked Congress to bestow a republican government on Alaska "with schools free to all, and with

equal laws, before which every citizen will stand erect in the consciousness of manhood. . . . Here will be a source of wealth more inexhaustible than any fisheries." [1]

According to a tradition steadfastly maintained by writers on Alaska who have only hastily examined the issue, Seward's move to acquire the region from Russia provoked a clamor of dissent and mockery. "Seward's Folly" was suggested for the territory's name, in competition with "Walrussia," and "Seward's Icebox," and Seward himself was vilified for buying a worthless piece of real estate. It is true that a few jokes were made and that there was some negative, politically-motivated criticism, but, on the whole, Americans reacted happily to the purchase. Editor James Gordon Bennett of the *New York Herald* printed a mock advertisement proclaiming that any European sovereign anxious to unload valueless land should apply to Seward—but even he favored the purchase. Americans believed in their Manifest Destiny and patriotic orators often called for the incorporation of all of North America into the United States.

Editorial writers praised Alaska. "Those who know most about it," stated the *Boston Herald,* "estimate it most highly. The climate on the Pacific side is not to be compared to that on the Atlantic side of the continent." But the country abounds in fur, forests, and minerals and "its waters swarm with fish." [2]

Another Boston newspaper pointed out the importance of the region to New England because of the "whale fishery of the North Pacific and Bering Strait, in which Massachusetts is so deeply interested." [3] The Bering Strait loomed on the consciousness of anyone concerned with whaling at that time because of the recent devastation of the New England whaling fleet by the Confederate raider *Shenandoah.* A chief Confederate objective during the Civil War had been the destruction of the Yankee whaling fleet, with its cargoes of valuable whale and walrus oil and ivory. The *Shenandoah,* commanded by Captain

1. Gruening, *An Alaskan Reader,* pp. 38–39, 40.

2. Richard E. Welch, Jr., "American Public Opinion and the Purchase of Russian America," in *Alaska and Its History,* edited by Morgan B. Sherwood (Seattle: University of Washington Press, 1967), p. 277.

3. Welch, "American Public Opinion," p. 278.

James I. Waddell, effectively accomplished that mission, catching the bulk of the Pacific whaling fleet in the Bering Sea and Bering Strait and destroying or holding for ransom thirty-eight ships with cargoes valued at $1,361,983. Though effective enough, the action took place after the Confederacy had fallen, a fact that Captain Waddell did not know until he learned it later, at sea, from a British ship in passage.

The *Shenandoah* episode alerted some editorialists to the strategic value of Alaska. One considered the region's location of greater value than the furs and fish it produced: "Of vastly more importance than all other things will be the command it will give us of the western and northwestern territory of this continent." [4] Developing the new country required care, cautioned the editor, but if done carefully the acquisition would compare with the Louisiana Purchase in significance.

Newspapers all over the country echoed the sentiments expressed in Boston and New York. Alaska was an exciting idea. It would have a great future. Few Americans cared to rush to Alaska to take part in the boom, but cheered on those who were going to make the territory realize its potential. One editor predicted that Sitka would boom in the manner of San Francisco. In ten years it would have fifty thousand people. Sitka has not yet come close to living up to that forecast, remaining a small town and a lovely one, ringed by forests and mountains and fronted by a beautiful bay dotted with evergreen islands.

The price for Alaska, as the *Boston Herald* reflected in April 1867, was dog cheap—there could be no doubt about it. Americans liked a bargain and calculations indicated that the acreage purchased from Russia came at a rock-bottom price: two cents an acre. Although the land had been there a long time, Americans did not know much about it. An effort from 1865 to 1867 by the Western Union Telegraph Company to construct a telegraph line through northern British Columbia to Alaska, thence across the Bering Strait to Siberia, focused some attention on the north. That colossal undertaking came to nothing; it was curtailed when Cyrus Field promoted the laying of a cable

4. Welch, "American Public Opinion," p. 278.

across the Atlantic to link Europe and North America by telegraph. With that achievement, any further work on an Alaskan-Siberian link became pointless.

Several members of the Western Union Telegraph Expedition contributed to the knowledge of Alaska. R. M. Banister, a scientist who left the North in 1866, briefed Massachusetts Senator Charles Sumner for the speech Sumner made in support of Secretary of State William Henry Seward's acquisition. Frederick Whymper, an English artist, and William Healy Dall, who was to become the leading scientist associated with Alaska's early American period, both published books on their experiences in the North. Whymper and Dall saw a good part of Russian America, because they took a canoe up the Yukon River into the interior, "one of the grandest streams on the North American continent," as Whymper observed, yet one that "has hitherto remained almost unnoticed." [5] Dall described "the noble stream extending 2,000 miles through a valley sometimes wide and low, sometimes narrow and contracted by low, wooded mountains." Apparently none of the river's many tributaries, some of which exceeded a thousand miles in length, had been explored. Most of the natives of the interior lived along the lower two-thirds of the river's length, from the Yukon mouth to the Tanana River. According to Dall's estimate, these natives numbered only two thousand to three thousand. The Russian traders maintained only three posts on the Yukon, manned chiefly by Creole servants of the company. The veneer of European culture was thinly spread, judging from the role of the church. One man wrote that "An inefficient priest, with a few alleged converts, conducted as a mission of the Greek church is the only religious establishement in the whole Yukon valley." [6]

Although the population of the great valley was sparse, resources were plentiful. Caribou and moose existed in large numbers. The migrating geese, ducks, and other fowl made the

---

5. Frederick Whymper, *Travel and Adventure in the Territory of Alaska* (New York: Harper and Bros., 1868), p. vii.

6. William Healy Dall, "Alaska as It Was and Is, 1865–1895," *Philosophical Society of Washington Bulletin* 13 (1895–1900): 131.

valley ring with their hoarse melodies. Rabbits, fox, lynx, wolves, wolverines, martens, otter, and other fur-bearing animals abounded. Runs of salmon and numerous other fishes along the Yukon and its tributaries endowed the region with a bountiful fishery. Salmon was a staple that could be preserved indefinitely as a hedge against hard times, and drying racks characterized the native fish camps along the river.

After the purchase, Congress established a Military District and a U.S. Customs District, extending the laws of customs, commerce, and navigation to Alaska. Placed in charge was a U.S. Army career officer whose first and last names were incredibly and improbably the same as those of the erstwhile president of the demolished Confederate States of America: General Jefferson C. Davis. The limited legislation provided the only law effective for the region until 1884, when Congress granted civil government. Military officers and their Alaskan charges protested vociferously against the indifference and inertia of Congress for that seventeen-year period. The military complained that they lacked authority to keep order and provide governance, and the residents cried that basic American rights of self-government and land ownership were being denied to them.

The army garrisoned at six posts in Alaska from 1867 to 1869: at Sitka, the former Russian capital; St. Paul, Kodiak Island, which had also been an important Russian-American Company center; Wrangell and Tongass in Southeastern Alaska, where any smuggling attempts from Canada could be thwarted; Kenai on Cook Inlet, where future settlement could be expected because the soil and climate seemed favorable; and on the Pribilof Islands to protect the fur-seal rookeries from the kind of indiscriminate killing by rival fur traders that had occurred after the transfer. Fur-seal pelt sales had sustained the Russians for years and were also the chief source of wealth in the early American period.

The army command understood its legal limitations. Major General H. W. Halleck, commanding the Military Division of the Pacific, "presumed that the transfer of this country will be followed by an organized territorial civil government with the extension over it of the general laws of the United States." [7] Against their will, officers had to assume civil powers to keep order, and it created an uncomfortable situation for them.

From his headquarters in Sitka, General Jefferson Davis consented to the formation of a municipal government for that settlement, and in November 1867 ninety-five voters elected a mayor and city council. The city council levied taxes on personal and real property and purchased a building for a schoolhouse. Some Sitka residents doubted the town government's legality and refused to pay taxes. This defiance, the dwindling of the economy, and the consequent exodus of many speculators who had hoped to make fortunes in Sitka doomed the municipal government after four years.

During its brief existence, Sitka's town government insisted it had no authority to punish capital crimes, and even the military hesitated to do so. A Creole murdered an Aleut woman in 1868, and General Davis's expedient was to send the killer to the Aleutians. In 1869, a man named J. C. Parker killed two Indians on separate occasions. Boards of army officers agreed each time that the killings were unjustified. Davis failed to arrest Parker after the first killing but did so after the second. After a few months Davis ordered his release at the request of the city council, and Parker escaped further punishment.

Army officers attacked the liquor problem with more decisiveness. From December 1872 to September 1875, the military arrested 148 civilians, most of them for being drunk and disorderly. Civilians were also locked up for fighting with or swindling Indians. Selling alcohol to Indians was punished, but liquor prohibition was impossible to enforce once the Indians learned how to make their own.

Even though the military acted to keep order in Sitka and in Wrangell after the Cassiar gold strike attracted numbers of prospectors in 1874, they resented the illegality of their position. As Captain J. B. Campbell put it in an 1876 report: "The commanding officer of Sitka is ordered both by the War Department and the headquarters department of Columbia, 'to proceed

7. Gruening, *An Alaskan Reader,* p. 34.

against persons violating the liquor laws of Congress.' '' Yet the commanding officer had no judicial power, ''and instructions as to what was meant by 'proceeding against' people were never received, although repeatedly asked for.'' Campbell had even queried the commanding general on the problem before taking up his assignment in Sitka. The general told him not to send prisoners to Oregon, since the courts there refused jurisdiction. What was he to do then? ''You must 'proceed against them' were the words, but no explanation was vouchsafed.'' [8]

Of the six garrisons stationed in Alaska the army closed all but Sitka's for reasons of economy by October 1870, although Wrangell's was reactivated in 1874 with the Cassiar gold rush. Troops were needed in the Northwest because of Indian unrest there and the Treasury Department insisted it could function in a manner superior to the army.

On the whole, the army proved to be wholly inadequate in colonial administration because of its lack of authority and experience. Furthermore, as a land-based force, it lacked the sea mobility necessary to policing a maritime environment. For most of its ten years' presence, its influence extended only to centers of white population, Sitka and Wrangell. The army showed no authority in the Arctic, south central or southwestern Alaska, or in the interior. In Sitka and Wrangell the army performed necessary functions of keeping order, dispensing relief provisions to the destitute, and maintaining sanitation, but it was certainly not a dynamic force for democratic progress in the transition period.

After the removal of the army in 1877, the Treasury Department took over the policing of Alaska. Its revenue cutters called sporadically at Sitka, Wrangell, and elsewhere in 1877 and 1878, but its officers were less effective than the army in keeping order. Drunkenness was endemic, and the few remaining whites in Sitka and Wrangell feared for their property and lives.

Violence broiled up in 1879 with the murder of a white miner by an Indian near Sitka. Other whites jailed the killer, but the Sitka Indians remonstrated. They demanded that the government compensate them for the loss of five natives who had been hired

8. U.S., Congress, Senate, *Military Arrests in Alaska,* 44th Cong., 1st sess., S. Ex. Doc. No. 33, 6 March 1876, p. 3.

the previous year by a white trader and had drowned in the Bering Sea. When the Indians grew drunk and riotous, the whites armed themselves and prepared their defenses. They also drew up a petition addressed to the British Royal Navy in British Columbia:

> We, the citizens of Sitka, Alaska, are now threatened with Massacre by Indians of this place. We have made application to Our Government for protection, which we hope will be extended, but the intricate forms of law through which our petition must drag its way will create delay, which may result in our entire demolition before the arrival of the necessary succor.[9]

The Sitkans begged for assistance and asked that "all forms of etiquette between governments" be laid aside, and "that you will take the side of an oppressed and threatened people." [10]

A passenger ship carried the appeal to Victoria, British Columbia, and Commander H. Holmes a'Court, captain of the H.M.S. *Osprey*, responded after securing approval from Washington. With the arrival of the *Osprey* and, a day later, a revenue cutter, things cooled down in Sitka, but the situation seemed serious enough that Commander a'Court agreed to remain until another revenue cutter reached Sitka.

Meanwhile American newspapers thundered against a government that so neglected its citizens. Some editorialists believed the explosiveness of the Sitkan situation had been exaggerated but, even so, it appeared that the government had been disgraced by the necessity of intervention by the Royal Navy. The *New York Times* urged the return of the army.

But now the U.S. Navy took its turn in Alaska. In March 1879, the U.S. *Alaska*, a steam sloop, voyaged to Sitka. A few months later the *Jamestown*, a full-rigged sailing ship commanded by Captain L. A. Beardslee, relieved the *Alaska*.

Beardslee criticized the Alaskans he encountered: "The general character of the whites was not such as would tend to produce or maintain in the Indians any great respect or fear, and

9. Bobby Lain, *North of Fifty-Three* (Ann Arbor: University Microfilms, 1974), p. 288.
10. Lain, *North of Fifty-Three,* p. 288.

they were regarded by them as outlaws and cast-offs of their own country." He reported "many of the Creoles being but little above the Indians in their qualifications and despised by them, while of the white settlers, the traders and saloon keepers were in strong opposition and in general hated each other cordially." [11]

Beardslee reported on the circumstances that had caused the Sitkan whites to appeal to the Royal Navy for help three months earlier. Before Beardslee's arrival, the Indian who had murdered the miner and started all the trouble in Sitka had been sent to Seattle and had been hanged there. Many Indians protested the execution to Beardslee. They understood the principles of a life for a life, but wondered at the unfairness of the proceedings. One Indian told the captain that "this man was hung upon the testimony of two of his enemies; he was in a strange country where he had no friends, and had he not been guilty it would have been all the same, he could not have proved it." [12] Other Indians protested the excessiveness of the punishment. Hanging was enough; why did the government then bury the victim's body? Burying was contrary to Indian tradition.

After soothing the ruffled sensibilities of Sitka's Indians and calming the fears of the whites, Beardslee voyaged to Wrangell, the only other settlement with a white community of any size. Missionaries had organized an Indian police force to keep order there. They had no legal authority to do so, yet it seemed a good answer to the law-and-order vacuum. The system worked well enough until January 1880, when visiting Hoochenoo Indians from Admiralty Island mixed up a fiery batch of distilled liquor (a specialty of these Indians, who learned the skill from soldiers and gave us the origin of the word *hootch*). The visitors neither knew nor cared that the Wrangell missionaries had banned the consumption of spirits, and they resented efforts of Indian police to arrest them. Shooting ensued, and the town's white residents were pinned down by the crossfire exchanged

11. U.S., Congress, Senate, *Report of Capt. L. A. Beardslee, U.S. Navy, Relative to Affairs in Alaska, and U.S.S. Jamestown . . .* , 47th Cong., 1st sess., Ex. Doc. No. 71, 24 January 1882, p. 13.

12. U.S., Congress, Senate, *Report of Capt. L. A. Beardslee*, p. 15.

between the two Indian forces. The Hoochenoos hurried away when they found themselves outgunned, but vowed to return with all their neighbors and execute bloody vengeance. Beardslee fixed up the dispute by giving military honors to chiefs of each tribe and even provided a peace-pipe—all of which were novelties to the Indians but diverting to them.

Beardslee tried to moderate the confusion of the Indians on the alcohol question. The customs collector at Sitka was adamant on the prohibition of all consumption of liquor by Indians. Yet cheap sugar or molasses, when combined with yeast and flour, and then distilled, produced a pleasant rum. Whites could buy liquor in Sitka, some Indians protested, so why should Indians not be permitted to drink? And why could one buy molasses for eating and not for distilling?

Seeing the rationality of the Indians' position, Beardslee allowed them to distill and drink. Native policemen were told to overlook stills and arrest public drunks only. Soon after the reform, the captain's police chief and the other Indians conducted a roaring, all-night binge. Beardslee instituted prohibition once more to keep the peace.

Beardslee knew he was subject to civil suits in arresting and confining Alaskans, but he was determined to control unruly whites and Indians, regardless of the state of the law. When the brig of the *Jamestown* overflowed with prisoners, he reopened the army guardhouse in Sitka and assigned marines to act as jailers. He shifted some of the civic burden to civilians by encouraging the formation of a local government in Sitka that would be empowered to regulate the liquor traffic. Voters elected a city council and a magistrate, but Beardslee's extralegal government proved to be impractical.

The captain and his successors performed well in keeping order among the Panhandle natives. They ignored the rest of Alaska, however. One commander reported in 1882 that "everything is quiet throughout the Territory of Alaska"—although his actual observation was limited to the southeastern part of the territory.[13]

One act of pacification under naval rule deserves mention because the issues involved have been revised and resolved only

13. Lain, *North of Fifty-Three*, p. 271.

recently. In 1882 one of the natives who hunted whales for a white concern based on Admiralty Island was killed when a harpoon head exploded. Other Indians seized two white men as hostages and demanded two hundred blankets for restitution. The navy swiftly dispatched a seventy-man force to Admiralty and, along the way, accepted the assistance of the revenue cutter *Corwin*. The navy commander issued a counterdemand for four hundred blankets. When the Indians refused to comply, the *Corwin* fired on the Indian village of Angoon, after determining that the women and children had been evacuated. A landing party then destroyed the Indians' canoes and burned twenty of the village's twenty-nine houses, leaving just enough housing to protect the natives over the winter. The Indians did not defend their homes and meekly accepted the admonishment of the naval officer—but they did not forget about the damage done to them. Their descendants filed claims against the United States government, and in 1974 they were awarded $90,000.

The United States government followed the precedent of the Russians in restricting the importation of firearms and "ardent spirits" to Alaska. American whalers and coastal traders violated the ban during the Russian era because smuggling paid well and enforcement was virtually impossible. After the purchase, smuggling thrived even more, for the same reasons.

Customs inspectors assigned to Alaska faced a staggering task. A handful of men were expected to police the vast territory. The southeastern Panhandle formed a smuggler's paradise with its thousand-mile-long inland waterway broken up by hundreds of islands, coves, and inlets. Officials did not even have adequate transport. One deputy stationed at Wrangell from 1871 to 1877 complained that he had nothing to do but "watch canoes pass and repass with smuggled goods." More than a decade later, Alaska's governor observed that the enforcement ability of customs officers was a bad joke: "There is no water patrol, no revenue cutter, no transportation, not even a row-boat . . . and as a consequence the smuggler pursues his nefarious calling with very little molestation from any quarter." [14]

14. Roland L. De Lorne, "Liquor-Smuggling in Alaska, 1867–1879," *Pacific Northwest Quarterly*, October 1975, p. 146.

Coastal residents bought liquor from passenger-ship seamen, whaling men, Indians who plied between Alaskan and Canadian communities by canoe, and from skippers of the numerous small schooners operating out of Canadian ports. Officers tried to regulate the traffic in the southeastern Panhandle, but had to ignore the rest of Alaska. No custom surveillance existed along the fifteen-hundred-mile coastline between Valdez and Unalaska on the Aleutian chain; and, except for an annual voyage after 1880, the revenue service did not police the Bering Sea or Arctic coasts.

Occasionally, officers apprehended smugglers. One of the more notorious operators was a popular ship captain, James Carroll. He carried opium from British Columbia to Alaskan ports for years before his ship was seized and searched at Port Townsend, Washington, in 1885. Agents poked around for six days and found 629 pounds of opium. The discovery represented merely the tip of the iceberg, as agents learned when they followed Carroll north to Kasaan and raided his warehouse there, to seize another 3,000 pounds of opium. Carroll was tried and fined, but his reputation did not suffer. He continued to command Alaskan ships and in 1889 was sent to Washington, D.C., by Alaskans who had a particular plea. Carroll told congressmen that new, fast revenue cutters were not needed in the North because smugglers used slow-moving canoes.

Sometimes bribed customs officials looked the other way when smugglers unloaded and vended contraband liquor. But even when they were able and willing to do their duty, they could not easily secure convictions. Successful prosecutions usually depended upon Indian witnesses, and white juries disdained their testimony—particularly as they considered prohibition to be unjust and irrational. Alaskans flouted the law openly, and the customs officials seemed impotent. One official complained in 1889 that twenty saloons ran busily in Juneau, eight in Sitka, five at Wrangell, and several others served drinks in Douglas and Chilkat.

For years, territorial officials urged the government to recognize that liquor prohibition was unenforceable in Alaska. Congress finally acted, in 1899, to replace prohibition with a license system. When thousands of gold-rushers poured into Alaska after the Klondike strike of 1897, the government was forced to note the helplessness of customs officials and so terminated a thirty-two-year episode of misrule and defiance.

Missionaries did as much to keep order among Alaskan natives as did government officials. The first Protestant mission and school in Alaska was founded in 1876 at Wrangell. When Dr. Sheldon Jackson, the ambitious missionary superintendent of the Rocky Mountain Presbytery of the Presbyterian Church, heard about the Alaskan mission, he determined to bring Alaska within his division. Indian education was only one part of his responsibility, but it held the highest interest for him. As he put it: "Most hypnotic of all was the persuasive mixture of service and power in the call to lift up the white man's burden." [15]

Jackson's first visit to Alaska in 1877 was a short one, but he soon returned with other missionaries and plans for the establishment of other schools and missions. His efforts received a good deal of U.S. government support after 1884, when he was appointed special agent in Alaska for the Bureau of Education. That role, which in his mind did not conflict with his other position as director of Presbyterian mission schools, enabled him to impose his policies for Indian education.

Jackson was not the most tactful of men and did not tolerate opposition to his methods. At Sitka he clashed with civil authorities who protested that Jackson was rounding up girls for a boarding school despite the disapproval of their parents. For a brief period, Sitka authorities held Jackson under arrest but were not able to curb the man's vision. The development of boarding schools had been initiated at Wrangell by another missionary who wanted to protect school girls from the predatory attentions of amorous miners. Jackson strove for the same goal at Sitka, as well; but, more generally, he focused on day schools that stressed industrial education on the model of the Carlisle School in Pennsylvania.

In 1890 Jackson made his first voyage north of the Aleutians to assist missionaries who were to establish the first Arctic

15. Maurice R. Montgomery, "An Arctic Murder" (Master's thesis, University of Oregon, 1963), p. 80.

schools at Point Hope, at Barrow, and on the Seward Peninsula at Cape Prince of Wales. He depended for transport upon the only government agency known in the North—the U.S. Revenue Marine. At every Eskimo village called at by the Revenue Marine ship, the signs of famine and destitution were prominent. Entire villages had been depopulated because of starvation. Heavy hunting of the caribou for trade with whalers had made the land animals scarce while the number of whales and walrus had been sharply decreased by the whalemen themselves. Jackson assumed that the Eskimos' condition was due to starvation alone, but it is more likely that such imported diseases as influenza, measles, and tuberculosis were the chief killers.

Jackson sent the first missionaries to the Arctic in 1890. Harrison R. Thornton and William T. Lopp established themselves at Cape Prince of Wales, a village of five hundred souls located at the extreme tip of Northwestern America. That first contact led to violence, and in that, the encounter was atypical in the missionary experience.

The two young Presbyterian ministers tended to brandish their Winchesters nervously when the villagers demanded entry to the little house that had been swiftly erected. It was not the custom to refuse entry to neighbors in Eskimo society, and the people were amazed to meet a bolted door when they wished to satisfy their curiosity. Lopp and Thornton hoped to express their trust and affection, but they were wary because of a violent episode in the history of Wales. There had been very few violent encounters between whites and Eskimos in the Arctic, but a few years prior to the founding of the Wales mission, whaling seamen killed some thirty Eskimos. The Wales Eskimos had boarded a ship for trade and frolic—as was the custom—and things got out of hand. Probably the Eskimos imbibed whiskey too freely, grew bold, and refused to leave the ship when ordered to do so. The New England whaling men panicked and resorted to force. The result was a massacre of all those who were not able to escape. Thus the apprehensions of Lopp and Thornton. Lopp conquered his fears and proved his capability. He was to have a lifelong career in religious and educational work in Alaska. Thornton was not so versatile, yet he tried hard at first. He joined the men in hunting seals and tried to be a good fellow. He managed to contain his rage when the hunters offered him a choice of young girls to complete his mock puberty rites after he had shot his first seal. He consented to rub noses with the seal and smear blood on his cheeks, but he "intended to remain loyal to the women" of his own country. Thornton relaxed his fear of the Eskimos of Wales after a time. His wife joined him there, and her company was a great benefit. He was optimistic concerning his endeavor. The Eskimos would surely accept the Christian message because they had no doctrine themselves to combat it with. For all practical purposes, their minds were "fallow for the reception of the good seed." Early missionaries generally downgraded the native culture and strove mightily to eradicate customs that they neither appreciated nor understood, but considered a threat to their mission. After two years among Eskimos, Thornton's doubts began to grow. He could not record a single case of conversion, and the Eskimos seemed to have derived no benefits from the missionaries' presence. Progress "in the virtues that make toward civilization and godliness" was so slow as to be meaningless.[16] Thornton reacted by becoming querulous. He grew weary of the Eskimos' pestering, their endless requests for matches, nails, and other trade items, and their insistence upon interrupting him with their demands and conversation.

Two boys brought Thornton's mission to its end. The young Eskimos were unusual in having a propensity for thievery. Several times they broke into the schoolhouse and pilfered things. Thornton could not handle them. He threatened and blustered and declared that he would shoot the thieves if they erred again. He carried his revolver with him at all times and, after a rifle shot was taken at him, he doubted that he would survive.

The boys found a loaded whaling gun on the beach and carried it to the missionary's cabin. When Thornton responded to a knock on the door, the boys blew a hole in his chest. To complete this grisly cycle of frontier horrors, the men of Wales,

16. Montgomery, "Arctic Murder," p. 82.

fearing that the guns of the U.S. revenue cutter *Bear* would smash their hovels, shot the two young murderers and laid their bodies at Mrs. Thornton's feet. To her credit, she asked the commander of the *Bear* to spare the village.

It should be emphasized that the tragic confrontation at Wales was abnormal. Generally, the missionaries, whether Protestant, Roman Catholic, or Orthodox, were revered. It is not easy to assess efforts of the missionaries. Clearly, they were powerful agents of disruption of the aboriginal culture. Yet disrupting contacts with white traders, explorers, or whalemen always occurred before missionaries were established in a particular area. They strove to uproot shamanism and any other beliefs and rituals that threatened Christian doctrine; and mostly they tried to eradicate the native language as well. On the other hand, the missionaries were often the only defenders of natives against the exploitation and the debauchery that other whites offered them. Missionaries acted as teachers, and sometimes as physicians, and recorded valuable observations of a changing culture.

But, except for a few instances of concern, law and order were not overwhelming concerns for Alaskans. What troubled them interminably was the need of a stronger economy. How could the great resources of the region be tapped in a way that would provide long-range support and insure continued development?

4

The Fur Frontier

*W*HEN Charles Sumner urged his colleagues in the United States Senate to ratify the purchase of Alaska, he catalogued the natural wealth of the territory: "the vegetable products . . . chief among which are forests of pine and fir waiting for the axe." The minerals—coal, copper, silver, lead, gold, granite—were abundant. And ice had already been exported from Alaska. Then there were "the furs, including precious skins of the black fox and sea-otter, which originally tempted the settlement . . . and, lastly, the fisheries, which, in waters superabundant with animal life beyond any of the globe, seem to promise a new commerce." [1] All of the resources praised by Sumner were to be exploited by Americans, although not in the order he listed, nor with the ease that his comments suggested.

The history of Alaska's resource utilization reveals the persistence of particular problems from the purchase to the present. Great distances, a severe climate in parts of the territory, a small population, a scarcity of capital investment, and adverse governmental policies have retarded Alaska's economic development. It was always easy to see that Alaska needed a stable economic base, an industry capable of attracting settlement and benefiting the resident population. But such a goal was difficult to realize. The fur industry was short-lived and primarily of

1. Gruening, *An Alaskan Reader,* pp. 38–39.

benefit to merchants in San Francisco. Gold production remained of bonanza proportions for only a few years, although corporations utilizing dredges operated until World War II, some working even through the 1950s. Lack of transport facilities and government land withdrawals hindered the mining of coal and other minerals and, for long, Alaska's timber did not attract investment. Profits from the abundant fisheries described so felicitously by Sumner ended in the pockets of Seattle-based cannery owners and fisheries.

Alaskans and, at times, outside commercial interests assumed that the federal government was obliged to assist development. Washington officials never held clear ideas on the extent of the government's responsibility. The government spent money prodigiously in the excitement of the gold rush and that of World War II, but spent little when Alaska did not command attention.

Alaskans complained when other national priorities overshadowed their needs. They often assumed that the government was neglecting them unjustly. Actually, it was a matter of interest rather than justice. Washington acted when it seemed urgent to foster a resource and, as may be expected, such action could be untimely, ill-conceived, or bungled in execution.

Within that framework of the government's relationship to Alaska, the logistics hindering development, and the dominance of resource exploitation by outside interests, we can understand the generally slow pace of development.

Substantial capital investment was slow to come to Alaska. In the early 1850s, California merchants risked a modest amount in an obvious resource—Alaska's ice—and began an enterprise that lasted for some thirty years. All of the ice consumed in California until the 1850s came by ship around the Horn from the east coast, which drove the cost prohibitively high. To gain a cheaper source of ice, businessmen in San Francisco formed the American Russian Commercial Company, commonly called the Ice Company, and negotiated with the Russian American Company in 1851 for the right to gather ice for shipment to the south. Aside from fur-gathering and whale hunting, the ice business was the first exploitation of a northern resource by Americans. It was a successful venture, too: 250 tons brought seventy-five dollars per ton in 1852.

A pond in Sitka initially provided ice for California. Blocks were cut, packed well in sawdust, and stored in ice houses until cargo ships reached the port and loaded the ice. Because of the need for sawdust, Sitka became the site of Alaska's first saw-mill. In the company's second year, the Sitka winter proved too warm, so that ice was taken from Baird Glacier, north of Peters-burg. The Ice Company moved to Kodiak the next season, built another sawmill, imported horses for hauling, and raised oats for feed. Kodiak's horses and oat-growing were, like the saw-mill operations, firsts for Alaska.

Ice shipments continued until 1880 when the company sus-pended operation. It was not for want of ice that the business ceased—ice was a prolifically renewable resource—but because its shipment became uneconomical. By 1880, Californians could buy inexpensive ice made by machines or natural ice hauled from the Sierra Mountains on the newly completed trans-continental railroad.

By the time at which the ice industry folded, another indus-try, on a scale much more vast than ice marketing, was expand-ing rapidly in Alaska. Fur-bearing sea and land mammals had always provided most of Alaska's wealth. In 1867, they drew the first substantial capital investment of the American era. In time, the development of the fisheries, particularly the salmon fisheries, came to overshadow the fur industry, but in Alaska's early years as American territory, furs produced most of the area's wealth.

San Francisco businessmen formed the Alaska Commercial Company—originally the Hutchison-Kohl Company—and pur-chased the assets of the Russian-American Company in 1867. For $155,000 the company acquired Russian ships, merchan-dise, and buildings in Sitka and the Pribilof Islands. Fur exploi-tation commenced in rousing form as the company tried to ex-pel other rival American traders from the Pribilofs. Traders had rushed to the teeming Pribilof rookeries to reap the harvest there. The Pribilof Islands of St. Paul and St. George, with the

Commander Islands off Kamchatka, offer the world's major breeding grounds for the fur seal. Fur-seal pelts did not command the prices of the sea otter, but the latter were virtually extinct by 1867.

To settle the squabbling of the traders over the fur seals, Congress prohibited the killing of fur seals in 1870, then called for bids from traders willing to lease the Pribilof Islands to take furs under government supervision. The Alaska Commercial Company bid successfully on the Pribilof lease and also contracted with the Russians for exclusive rights to the fur seals of the Commander Islands.

The company's twenty-year lease allowed them to kill 100,000 animals every year in return for a yearly rental fee of $55,000 and a revenue tax of $2.63 for each skin taken. The lease stipulated that Aleut residents of the island must be hired to kill and skin the seals at a rate of forty cents per seal. In addition, the company must provide free housing, schooling, and some provisions for the Aleuts. The arrangement was unusual in America's frontier history, but it seemed satisfactory to all concerned—except for the San Francisco fur-trade rivals of the successful bidders.

The company also took over the fur trade of the interior, notably that of the Russian posts at St. Michael, near the mouth of the Yukon River, and Nulato, six hundred miles upstream. Trading for furs in the interior was open to anyone, but the company had little competition because transportation was difficult. The Alaska Commercial Company handled its own shipping. Until the gold-rush era, the company maintained the only regular ocean service between San Francisco and St. Michael, and the only steamers plying the Yukon River.

For the twenty-year lease period, the Alaska Commercial Company thrived in the fur trade. Shareholders received handsome dividends and hoped that they could maintain their near-monopoly of Alaska's trade. The company enjoyed its comfortable arrangement with the government and did not urge Washington to undertake any development. In fact, it seemed to be the company's policy to play down Alaska's economic potential.

The writings of naturalist Henry Wood Elliott expressed best an attitude that could be called an anti-Alaska campaign. It is not clear whether Elliott was paid by the company for extolling its island operation and damning the rest of Alaska, but his sentiments were certainly supportive of company interests. Elliott had lived on the Pribilofs from 1872 to 1874 to study fur seals, and he observed there "the perfect working of an anomalous industry, conducted without a parallel in the history of human enterprise, and of immense pecuniary and biological value." [2]

Elliott found perfect conditions on the Pribilofs but saw only bleakness for the economic future elsewhere in the North. He argued that the climate would always inhibit development and "unfit the Territory for the proper support of any considerable population." Not that it mattered for the destiny of the United States: "There are more acres of better land lying now as wilderness and jungles in sight on the mountain tops from the car windows of the Pennsylvania railroad than can be found in all Alaska." Supporters of Alaska's potential attacked Elliott viciously after his book, *Our Arctic Province,* appeared in 1886, but he did not back down. In an article in *Harper's,* he stressed the positive side: "Though we know now that Alaska will never be, in all human probability, the land for us, yet we have one great comfort in its contemplation, for we shall never be obliged to maintain costly mail routes or appoint the ubiquitous postmaster here." Elliott offered other comforting predictions. American taxpayers need not fear that Alaska's maintenance would cost them anything. Even such basic facilities as navigational aids were unnecessary: "Much as the coast looms upon the map, we shall never have to provide lighthouses for its vacant harbours." [3]

Elliott derided the efforts of the Americans who rushed to Sitka in 1867 to exploit the new territory:

> A decade has elapsed since the doublecrested eagle flew from the dreary length and chilly breadth of Alaska, and during that time the

2. Henry Wood Elliott, *Our Arctic Province: Alaska and the Seal Islands* (London: Sampson, Low; New York: Charles Scribner's Sons, 1886), p. 189.

3. Henry Wood Elliott, "Ten Years' Acquaintance with Alaska," *Harper's,* November 1877, pp. 815, 816.

intense materialistic eyes of our fellow-citizens have been keenly
scrutinizing the rugged land, the timber thicket, the furry beasts,
and finny visitants that are purely and essentially Alaskan, with the
undisguised determination to strike in at once where it would pay.[4]

The writer likened America's approach to the newly purchased territory to the manner of a boy who, when presented
with a strange toy, tries to investigate its inner workings and
then, in time, lays it aside. Americans "pitied the ignorance"
of the Russians who were so preoccupied with furs that they
could not know of anything else of value in Alaska; yet, after
ten years of "careful inquiry, we find, too, that we today 'don't
know of anything else'." There are marginal benefits, of
course. "Though we have lost the wild apples at Sitka, and
have failed to see the shimmer of golden fields of corn at Kodiak, yet we have much to please and far more to interest us in
Alaska," Elliott wrote. The area was a paradise for naturalists,
a "happy hunting ground" for the ethnologist, a new and
boundless field for the geologist, "and the physical phenomena
of its climate are something wonderful to contemplate." For
years to come it would be a treasure-trove for these scientists,
"but, alas! it bids fair, from what we now know, never to be a
treasure-trove for the miner or the agriculturist." [5]

Elliott could also confess to some knowledge of human nature. He had still another rationalization for economy and sim-
plicity. "We have learned enough of the country and climate by
this time to know that the lands and fishing waters now occupied by the natives of Alaska will never be objects for the cu-
pidity of our people." It followed that "as the Indians then are
undisturbed, they in turn are not going to disturb us, and the
subject of maintaining law and order there becomes a very simple one indeed, and inexpensive." All that the government had
to do was "to suppress all agencies which tend to debauch and
ruin them and their hunting industries." [6] In other words, keep
booze sellers away from the natives, and they will support

    4. Elliott, "Ten Years' Acquaintance," p. 801.
    5. Elliott, "Ten Years' Acquaintance," p. 801.
    6. Elliott, "Ten Years' Acquaintance," p. 803.

themselves without any drain on the taxpayers of the United States.

That, in fact, was the government's policy, even before Elliott ventured to the North. He was merely condoning the status quo.

Governor Alfred P. Swineford counted among the men whose belief in Alaska's potential conflicted sharply with Elliott's— and with that of fur traders, as well. Swineford was appointed governor in 1885, following the very short term of the territory's first governor, John Henry Kinkead, who had been appointed in 1884 by President Chester A. Arthur. In his first annual report, Swineford highlighted the needs and the value of Alaska. He reported that outside interests owned all the canneries and that operators employed outside workers, often Chinese. The only industry that provided any tax benefit to Alaska was mining, and it had not yet developed to substantial proportions. Swineford described the territory as "a national fat goose left unprotected and . . . annually plucked of its valuable plummage [*sic*] by non-resident corporations." [7]

Swineford believed that out of fear of taxation the Alaska Commercial Company conspired to keep Congress from providing for Alaska. Swineford charged that Elliott was a paid lobbyist of the Alaska Commercial Company and asked that *bona fide* residents be heard from rather than "the willful misrepresentations of the hired assassins of her progress and welfare who infest the national capital during its every session." In a subsequent report, Swineford even more directly blamed Elliott and the fur dealers for convincing Congress that they need not concern themselves with Alaska. The fur monopoly had been responsible for "defeating nearly every proposed act of legislation calculated to insure the settlement and development of Alaska." He charged the company with "a studied and determined effort" to convince the government and the public that Alaska's only value lay in its fur-bearing animals. "Agents of the government," he wrote, "sent out to examine and report upon its

7. Ernest Gruening, *The State of Alaska,* revised edition (New York: Random House, 1968), p. 65.

resources, instead of honestly performing the service for which they were paid, have, in the interest of a corporation into whose service they have drifted . . . broadcast statements concerning the climate and undeveloped resources of Alaska which they knew were utterly false, but which, according with a preconceived public opinion born of ignorance, were generally accepted as true.'' [8]

The opposing views of Alaska Commercial Company spokesmen and Swineford were irreconcilable in their day and have not been resolved yet. In later decades, other antagonists were to dispute the question of Alaska's potentials and needs in similar terms. Always the focus has been on either the government's obligations in the development of Alaska's resources, or on the question of whether the resources should be developed at all. The Bering Sea fur-seal controversy drew the world's attention to the necessity for resource conservation and resulted in a pioneering treaty on conservation.

The dispute arose when hunters began to kill large numbers of fur seals as the animals migrated along the northwest coast on the way to their breeding grounds on the Pribilofs. In 1870 small schooners out of San Francisco and Victoria, British Columbia, outfitted for pelagic—or high-seas—hunting for the first time. Hunters watched for seals off the Washington coast, then followed them north, killing all the way. Pelagic hunting was profitable; the schooner fleet increased from 16 in 1870 to 34 in 1883, when the hunters first went into the Bering Sea, to 115 in 1889. Their catches increased from 15,000 seals in 1882 to 60,000 by 1895. Many more seals were shot than were taken because it was not easy to recover the animals at sea. The wastage was particularly conspicuous.

Naturally, the Alaska Commercial Company grew alarmed at the effects of pelagic sealing on their Pribilof industry. That was one situation in which the company wanted government intervention. Because of the company's political influence and the emotionalism generated by the issue, the government directed the U.S. Revenue Marine Service to arrest pelagic sealers in the

8. Gruening, *State of Alaska,* pp. 69–70.

Bering Sea. In 1886 three Canadian schooners were seized and taken to Sitka. At once Britain protested that action as violation of her freedom of the seas. The American government claimed the right of seizure on grounds that the Bering Sea was within United States territorial sovereignty. American diplomats insisted that Russia had claimed sovereignty over the North Pacific in 1821 and that the United States had inherited Russian rights. British diplomats reminded their counterparts that in 1821 the U.S. government had stridently protested the Russian claims of sovereignty and had subsequently disregarded them.

The British were not sure whether the American diplomats were ignorant of past events or preferred to suppress the truth. One writer in the English journal *Fortnightly Review* thought that the American public "could not be expected to swallow such a preposterous claim with credulity so the pill was sugared with much talk about humanity to seals and the need of protecting the herd against extermination." [9]

The controversy over the fur seal raged for several years. British and American scientists investigated the Pribilof herds several times, disputing the populations of the rookeries and the most effective means of conserving the mammals. Britain contended that it seemed unreasonable for Americans to call for the elimination of high-seas hunting while permitting the seasonal seal slaughter on the islands. Americans argued that the island killing could be controlled and was not wasteful.

In 1889, Britain and the United States agreed to submit the issue for arbitration. In 1893 the Paris Arbitration Tribunal rejected the American claim to Bering Sea sovereignty but also ruled against pelagic sealing. A sixty-mile protected zone was established around the islands; sealing during the months of migration was prohibited, as was the use of firearms.

Later, in 1911, the United States formulated treaties with Britain and Japan, permitting those nations to have 15 percent of the skins taken on the Pribilofs or an equal value in cash.

Some Americans were incensed at the arbitration agreement. "It is not a page of American diplomacy upon which we can

9. H. W. Wilson, "Bering Sea Controversy," *Fortnightly Review*, October 1896, p. 682.

look back in pride; but it offers the most wholesome lesson,"
wrote Theodore Roosevelt in 1895. "It should teach us to be-
ware, beyond all others, of the peace-at-any-price men." Roosevelt was staunchly insistent. "Above all, it should teach us
the lesson of courteous but resolute insistence on our *rights*, AT
NO MATTER WHAT COST." [10]

Congress was unhappy with the wrangling over the treaties
for conservation of the seals. The House actually passed a bill
calling for the slaughter of all the seals on the Pribilofs. Such an
action would have enriched the U.S. Treasury by five million
dollars, and further cruel starvation of motherless seal pups
would have been prevented. In the Senate, however, the bill
failed to pass.

The Alaska Commercial Company lost its bid for a renewal
of the Pribilof lease in 1890 to a rival San Francisco trading
company. The set-back was not deeply felt because of the declining market for seal pelts and because other commercial prospects were stirring in the North. Furs could never attract many
to settle in Alaska, nor would the resource support substantial
communities. But mineral wealth could do both, if it existed in
large quantities, and particularly if the earth held precious met-
als such as gold.

10. Wilson, "Bering Sea Controversy," p. 679.

5

All the Glitter of Gold

IN 1869, during the fur-trade boom, the Alaska Commercial Company's steamer ascended the Yukon River to establish a fur-trading post at Nulato. Subsequently, the company founded other posts to attract natives to trade their furs for provisions and equipment. In opening the interior to trade, the company inadvertently provided the means by which Alaska's economic base shifted from furs to minerals. Gold prospectors first entered the Yukon Valley in the 1870s and began their long search for a bonanza. In a real sense, these men were transitional figures, since some of them doubled as traders for the company in order to earn their grubstakes. Thus the fur industry supported the incipient mineral industry.

The first major strike in Alaska occurred, not in the Yukon Valley, but at Juneau on the southeastern coast in 1880. A boom town swiftly developed there and attracted hundreds of hopeful argonauts. In the next twenty years, mines in southeastern Alaska produced $17,276,000 in gold. Some of the miners worked at Juneau's quartz or hard-rock mines just long enough to earn a grubstake, then pushed on into the interior by way of the Chilkoot Pass, to look for gold.

In 1886, miners struck a rich placer field on a tributary of the Forty Mile River in a region that straddled the Alaska-Yukon Territory border. The first interior gold town developed at Forty Mile in Canada, just twenty-five miles from the American bor-

der. In the decade following the Forty Mile discovery, the value
of Alaska-Yukon gold production rose from $30,000 in 1887 to
$800,000 in 1896.[1]

Mining methods at that time were primitive. No one had elab-
orate equipment. The bedrock upon which the gold was located
lay from twenty to two hundred feet under the ground, which
usually was frozen. To penetrate the permafrost, miners had to
burn out a shaft with wood fires. The tedious process of thawing, removing the dirt, then thawing again led finally to bedrock. Then miners hoisted the gold-bearing gravel to the surface in buckets and, in the summer months when water was
available, washed the gravel down in pans and sluice boxes to
separate the dirt from the gold.

Circle City became the first gold town of Alaska's interior. In
1893, gold seekers discovered the precious metal on Birch
Creek, 240 miles down the Yukon River from Forty Mile. Circle soon held several hundred residents housed in log cabins and
enjoyed the amenities of an Alaska Commercial Company store,
saloons, dance hall, opera house, and resident prostitutes. Regular steamboat service on the Yukon was established, as well.
Shallow-draft steamboats voyaged between St. Michael, near
the mouth of the Yukon, to Circle and beyond.

Late in 1896, gold was found on the Klondike, a tributary of
the upper Yukon within Canada. The greatest of the northern
stampedes followed, in 1897 and 1898, as some hundred thousand men and women started off for the North to reap its riches.
Dawson City was the glittering goal of most hopefuls who
crossed the Chilkoot or White passes from the coast at Skagway
or transferred from an ocean vessel to a steamboat at St. Michael to voyage up the Yukon. About forty thousand rushers
reached Dawson, and another ten thousand arrived in Alaska.
With so many thousands of prospectors in the country, gold
inevitably was to be discovered elsewhere. Major discoveries
after the Klondike occurred in Alaska, rather than Canada. In
1899 and 1900, the area of Nome on the coast of the Bering Sea

1. Alfred H. Brooks, *Blazing Alaska's Trails,* 2d edition (Fairbanks: University of
Alaska Press, 1973), p. 332. William R. Hunt's *North of 53°* (New York: Macmillan
Publishing Company, Inc., 1974) treats Alaska's mining history in detail.

boasted gold strikes. Miners made $2,152,000 the first season and more than $4,000,000 annually for the next several years.

Mining activity spread throughout the Seward Peninsula, but the next major gold discoveries were made in the Tanana Valley in 1902. There, deep in the interior, the town of Fairbanks grew to become the largest population center of the territory. As the first major Alaskan town to be founded away from the coast, Fairbanks had a tremendous impact on the development of the interior.

Soon after the Fairbanks strike, mining technology advanced in Alaska. In 1904, the first large dredge began operation at Nome. A dredge was able to scoop up bedrock gravel and wash it down automatically. Steam or water points driven into the ground thawed the earth, and powerful hydraulic hoses washed away the overlay of soil covering the bedrock before the dredge set to work.

Juneau, Nome, Fairbanks, and other smaller communities owed their existence to gold discoveries. These towns drew a permanent population from outside, and their stability—even after gold production declined—determined the continued development of Alaska. But for the stability of these towns and their influence on government and private investments, the territory could conceivably have drifted back to a pre-Klondike status after the gold was worked out.

Population figures express the significance of the gold rushes. In 1890, Alaska counted only 32,052 residents and, in 1900, almost twice that number—63,592, of whom 29,536 were natives. Ten years later, the population was about the same: 64,356.

In 1916, some 9,840 men were employed in mining, and Alaskan mineral production peaked that year at a total value of $48,632,138. By 1920, the number employed in mining had dwindled to 4,570. Production continued to fall during the depression. In 1931, the production total was $12,278,000; in 1933, it was $10,366,000. Gold values soared when President Franklin D. Roosevelt increased the price of gold from $20.67 to $35.00 an ounce in 1933. In 1934, gold production in Alaska reached a value of $16,007,000; and in 1940, it reached the record high of $26,178,000, most of it gathered by the forty-eight dredges operated that year.

World War II killed gold mining. Gold production was suspended as a nonessential industry in wartime, and gold mining was never able to make much of a comeback afterward. The recent increase in gold prices has stimulated a quickened interest in Alaska. One of the dredges at Nome that had not been operated for years is working once more, and there has been a little more mining and prospecting activity elsewhere in Alaska as well.

During the peak year for mineral production in Alaska—1916—$29,484,291 of the total production figure came from copper produced by the Kennecott mines of south-central Alaska. The Kennecott mines tapped one of the world's richest lodes of copper. Alaskan Indians had known of rich copper deposits along the upper Copper River rising in the Wrangell Mountains. They had brought it to the attention of, first, the Russians, and, later, the Americans. The area was difficult to reach and to explore because of river currents and glaciers near the river mouth. In 1908, however, J. P. Morgan and the Guggenheim family interests combined to form what Alaskans usually called the Alaska Syndicate, bought the valuable copper mines in that area, and began construction of a railroad from Cordova to the mines.

Except for a few short-line railroads serving gold-mining districts, the Alaska Syndicate's Copper River and Northwestern Railroad, built to serve the Kennecott copper mines, was the only railroad built in Alaska in the gold-rush era. The line ran from Cordova on the coast to the Chitina Valley, a distance of some 131 miles, then continued on another 65 miles to the mines. Building it had been a herculean task that had occupied five thousand men from 1907 to 1911. Glaciers, rivers, and mountains had to be overcome. The railroad cost $23 million to build; but before it was shut down in 1938, it had carried $200 million in copper and silver to the coast.

In addition to operating the Kennecott copper mines, the Alaska Syndicate also bought gold fields in various parts of the Yukon Territory and Alaska and carried out large-scale dredging operations. The Syndicate went into the salmon industry, as well, and established the Alaska Steamship Company, with a fleet of seventeen ships.

Alaskans accused the Syndicate of trying to strangle every enterprise it could not control. The editorial language used by the *Nome Gold Digger* in 1907 was typical, referring to the Syndicate as the "vampire which has already started its bloodsucking operation [and] is laying its plans for the complete subjection of the country to its will." [2]

Despite the phobias of Alaskans, it appears that the Syndicate did not differ, except in size, from any other outside business enterprise. It possessed the capital that Alaskans lacked to rework abandoned gold fields with dredges and to build a costly railroad to its copper mines. And like other cannery and shipping operators, the Syndicate lobbied in Washington against fish-pack taxes and gave preferential freight rates to its subsidiaries.

Residents of the new gold towns urgently demanded services of the federal government. Nothing ever seemed to be accomplished fast enough. Miners who stampeded to Nome in the summer of 1899 could not understand why the postal department could not arrange a mail service before the next spring. Travelers on the Valdez Trail in 1912 would unhitch their dogs or horses, stable them, then sit around the roadhouse stove and grouse about the government's neglect of the road. Businessmen in Fairbanks wondered why the government could not provide a railroad link through Canada to the United States. Look at all the gold we provide the treasury, they reflected, and notice how much money Uncle Sam is spending in the Philippines.

Various government agencies had responded to the Klondike stampede. The army explored various routes into the interior—though usually in the wake of eager prospectors, rather than in advance. The Revenue Marine patrolled the Yukon River, while the army made some belated efforts to assist beleaguered, outgunned civil officials to police such roaring towns as Skagway and Nome. Inertia in Washington was blamed for the un-

2. *Nome Gold Digger,* November 29, 1907.

ruly condition of these towns in the 1898–1900 period. Of all federal agencies, the postal service probably did the best job, considering the travails and distances involved, although the army's construction and operation of a telegraph system was also a distinguished achievement.

The government must also be credited for providing the first "all-American" route to the interior. Tremendous effort was expended to build a road into the interior from the coast. The call for such a road became urgent only with the gold stampedes. Prior to the 1897–1900 Klondike and Nome discoveries, the Yukon River, once the ice dashed out in spring, was highway enough to serve the small needs of interior dwellers. In 1899, the U.S. Army began building a trail from Valdez on Prince William Sound to Eagle, far up on the Yukon River, near the boundary with Canada's Yukon Territory. Some of the early arrivals at Fairbanks in 1904 came over a branch of the trail, and with the growth of Fairbanks, that route became the recognized one, and the segment to Eagle was abandoned. After 1909, improvements of the trail made horse-sled and wagon transport possible most of the year, and a regular stage service commenced.

But where are our railroads?—cried exasperated Alaskans. The government was slow to respond, presumably reasoning that private capital should finance railroads—an attitude encouraged by the visionaries who had always been certain that capital invested in large-scale northern projects could be recovered.

The government's reluctance to build railroads in Alaska angered the residents. "Aside from the deprivation of the people of Alaska of their rights of citizenship in their own country," wrote one editorialist, "the question of greatest moment in the development of Alaska is that of better and cheaper transportation." Something had to be done so that the "great resources" of the territory that were not located on tidewater could be made available. It was stunning to reflect on what a wealth of production awaited the construction of a railroad— "more than a hundred thousand square miles of agricultural lands, in addition to the lower-grade gold ores and gravel beds." [3] Resources abounded in the North and, once developed, a profitable employment for a large population was guaranteed—so prevailing sentiment ran.

Such statements and prophecies were typical. During the controversy over opening entry to coal lands, writers usually attacked conservationists. Railroads should be supported by "those who are talking so much of conservation." The resources of the North should be put to work. "Every year's delay means incalculable waste." [4]

In 1913, a territorial commission appointed to study and report on the best way to serve the interior by rail recommended two routes. One would utilize the Copper River and Northwestern Railroad route from Cordova, on the coast, to Chitina, then go on from there to Fairbanks. The other would commence in Seward, run to the Susitna Valley, then swing over to the Kuskokwim River. But eventually only one line was built, that from Seward via Anchorage to Fairbanks. President Woodrow Wilson chose that route over congressional delegate James Wickersham's objections that it was both impractical and uneconomical. The choice meant stagnation for the Cordova-Chitina region after the copper mines were worked out, but the train line also determined that the new railroad town of Anchorage would become Alaska's hub.

Congress authorized construction of the railroad in 1915. Construction was restricted to the summer seasons, and it was 1923 before the link of more than four hundred miles was completed.

From the time of Nome's founding in 1899–1900, Alaskans had dreamed of a railroad that would run from the states through Canada to the Seward Peninsula, cross the narrow fifty-six-mile gap of the Bering Strait, and then tie into the Trans-Siberian Railroad. John J. Healy, a pre-Klondike Alaskan trader who formed the North American Trading and Transportation Company in the 1890s to compete with the Alaska Commercial Company in servicing Yukon Valley gold miners, was the most

3. "Conservation," *Alaska-Yukon Magazine*, February 1912, pp. 57–58.
4. "Conservation," pp. 57–58.

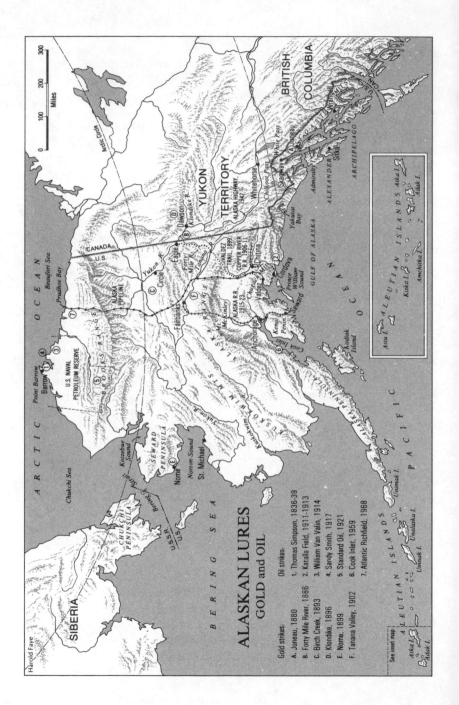

Harold Faye

ALASKAN LURES
GOLD and OIL

Gold strikes:

A. Juneau, 1880
B. Forty Mile River, 1886
C. Birch Creek, 1893
D. Klondike, 1896
E. Nome, 1899
F. Tanana Valley, 1902

Oil strikes:

1. Thomas Simpson, 1836-39
2. Katalla Field, 1911-1913
3. William Van Valin, 1914
4. Sandy Smith, 1917
5. Standard Oil, 1921
6. Cook Inlet, 1959
7. Atlantic Richfield, 1968

serious promoter of that visionary scheme. Healy announced his railroad plans in 1904 and dispatched a partner to Russia in quest of a concession to operate there. His hopes and those of Alaskans who would benefit from the railroad—particularly Nome residents—remained high through 1905 and 1906, although capital proved hard to raise. But in 1907, the czar's government firmly rejected a concession. Russians were more dissuaded than allured by what Americans envisioned for Siberian development should the two continents be connected by rail: it would not do to risk having Siberia become a colony of the United States.

A trans–Bering Strait railroad might have forced the pace of Alaska's economic development, or it might have become the most colossal white elephant of this century. But despite the failure of Healy's project, there were persistent economic relations between northeastern Siberia and northwestern Alaska. Trade between the two continents was brisk. And Alaska's reindeer industry, which grew into a unique meat-marketing enterprise, originated with stock shipped across the Bering Strait from Siberia.

6

Ties between Siberia
and Alaska

$\mathcal{T}$HE most persistent international contact in the North, the long-standing contact between northwestern Alaska and northeastern Asia through trade across the Bering Strait, has been little noticed by historians or diplomats, despite its color and interest.[1] Aborigines had maintained a trading pattern for hundreds of years before white men inhabited the North, establishing ample historic precedent for the kind of traffic that later developed. The modern phase of commercial traffic began with the founding of Nome in 1899. Nome was built at a frenzied pace during the gold rushes of 1899 and 1900, when some twenty-thousand argonauts flocked to the desolate, treeless shores of the Seward Peninsula. By 1905, the excitement had died down considerably, but the placer mines of the region produced steadily, and the town afforded all the cultural amenities—newspapers, theaters, churches—to be found in any bustling western community.

The Bering Strait, a mere fifty-six miles at its narrowest, separates the Seward Peninsula from northeastern Siberia. That geographic proximity suggested similar potentials to American

1. William R. Hunt's *Arctic Passage* (New York: Charles Scribner's Sons, 1975) treats the Bering Sea frontier in detail.

mining men and entrepreneurs. Miners expected that the miraculous yield of the "golden sands" of Nome could be duplicated in Siberia. After all, the two regions resembled each other in surface appearance and geological structure. In fact, thousands of years earlier, a land bridge had connected the two continents, providing a passage for early man's migrations from Asia to America. Traders, too, saw advantages in the nearness of Siberia. The czar's government neglected its distant provinces, and commercial links between European Russia and northeastern Siberia had always been very tenuous.

Yankees had stepped in to fill an obvious commercial need, long before the northern gold discoveries. The ships of the New England whaling fleet first began hunting in the Bering Sea in the mid-nineteenth century, and they customarily carried trade items in demand among Siberian natives. Firearms and liquor dominated the trade. In return, natives offered whalebone and furs, and some natives joined the American vessels for the Arctic Ocean segment of their cruise. Northeastern Siberian Chukchis and Eskimos spoke more English than Russian and were more familiar with Americans and their goods than with Russians. The demise of whaling in the late nineteenth century might have lessened American influence had it not been for the sudden booming of the town of Nome.

Two major links developed between Nome and Siberia. In 1902, a Seattle entrepreneur, John Rosene, organized the North Eastern Siberian Company to trade and prospect for gold. Rosene secured a concession to the Chukotsk Peninsula through a dummy partner who was a Russian nobleman. For several years the operation went along briskly. Parties of prospectors usually outfitted themselves in Nome. Nome's Chamber of Commerce had visions of a rosy economic future for their town, which was then the only large settlement on either side of the Bering Sea. But, alas, Rosene failed to find gold in Siberia. In 1909, he gave up both mining and storekeeping.

But an important trading link remained lively. A number of daring skippers whose little schooners made up the "mosquito fleet" of Nome carried on trade. These sea dogs were daring, not so much in their perilous navigation of ice-strewn, storm-lashed waters—which was hazardous enough—but in their challenge of Russian authority. The Russians tolerated the Nome trade, but did not encourage it to the extent of providing a customs station north of Petropavlovsk on the Kamchatka Peninsula. Disdaining the long voyage to Kamchatka and the payment of license fees, most Nome traders took their chances with the Russian patrol vessels. Usually, trading schooners evaded the two vessels patrolling the waters.

Nome traders avoided Russian officials for another reason: more often than not, the Americans carried a contraband cargo. Booze was a most desirable trade item in the twentieth century, as it had been earlier, and its exchange greatly augmented profits. Nome's newspaper boosted the prospects of the Siberian trade at every opportunity, although it cautioned against dealing in liquor.

The Bering Sea neighbors had a history of good relations. Russian patrol boats often called at Nome, and officers entertained Americans aboard their ships and went ashore to be feasted in return. It was the same when U.S. Revenue Cutter Service vessels called at Siberian towns. Mutual hospitality and aid was generously proffered. Sometimes language caused a little difficulty, but good fellowship and bountiful toasts eased the strain.

But that era of friendship passed with the Russian Revolution of 1917. For several years, supporters of the revolution battled followers of the czar. Trading activity slowed down in 1917 and 1918, but picked up again in 1919. The *Nome Nugget,* the town's newspaper, predicted that year that Nome merchants would sell supplies and fuel of a value close to six figures to Siberian traders. The Karieff brothers, Russians who had stations in northern Siberia, led the field, but Nome schooners worked the Siberian coast as well—among them the *Belvedere, Noatak, Trader, Flyer, Alaska, Nugget, Belinda, Polar Bear,* and *Jewel Guard.*

Trade exceeded the expectations of Nome merchants in 1919. By September 1, it appeared that Nome would provide up to $500,000 worth of goods to Siberian traders. Boosters surely believed that that volume would be doubled or trebled within the next two years. Geographic logic provided the base for such optimism. Northeastern Siberia's population of about fifty thousand people depended upon the centers of Petropavlovsk and Nome. Nome's proximity to most of the villages permitted its traders to offer cheaper prices, shorter waits, and a greater variety of goods. Siberians would welcome improvements in the service Nome offered, and Nome's commercial leaders knew exactly how the government could help out: they asked U.S. postal officers to establish direct mail and telegraph communications across the Bering Strait. Such a service would do a great deal to further Nome's commercial hegemony over northeastern Siberia. The American government had built on the Snake River a small boat harbor that provided protection to the schooners of the Siberian trade and that had been a stimulant to Siberian merchants. Mail service would surely spark activity further. Russian businessmen assured the Nome people that more Russian ships could be expected to call.

During the same season, some speculative trade took place. The Russian gunboat *Yakut* called at Nome in September and its 145-man crew went ashore. Because of the civil strife in Russia, it was not clear which of the currencies, czarist, Kolchak, Bolshevik, or others, would eventually be recognized as standard. Some Nome merchants accepted czarist roubles at eighteen to a dollar rather than at the normal two-to-one ratio. Even at that, the Americans lost money.

As the ice went out of the Bering Sea in 1920, it seemed to many as if a new era were dawning for the Bering Sea frontier. The year 1919 had been an extremely successful trade year, and many signs now pointed toward favorable changes. But the "new era" was not viewed in the same light on both sides of the sea. In Nome, enthusiasm ran high for an acceleration of Siberian and Alaskan Arctic exploitation. The *Nome Nugget* even added a slogan to its front page, proclaiming in each issue that "NOME IS THE DISTRIBUTING CENTER AND GATEWAY TO NORTHERN ALASKA AND SIBERIA." That had been true for twenty years; why should not the relationship be developed even further in the future?

Unfortunately, an impediment to the program Alaskans had

hoped for threatened, as stern warnings were issued from Siberia. The Bolsheviks, although still not firmly in control of northeastern Siberia, began asserting the intent of the new regime—and that caused gloom in Nome. The Red Revolution had not received a very good press anywhere in America, and the Alaskans of Seward Peninsula, who were sure they knew the Bolsheviks better than any of their countrymen did, feared the worst for their commercial prospects. Regulations announced from Anadyr, Siberia, did not seem so onerous to those not involved in the trade. Vessels from Nome were required to call at Anadyr each season for a license and had to carry someone proficient in Russian among the crew. Traders grumbled that too few Russian-language speakers lived in Nome, making it difficult to meet the requirement. But they were much more incensed by the license requirement itself, though they said publicly that the impracticality of a call at Anadyr before trading to the North disturbed them most. Some schooners had such limited fuel capacity that they had to return to Nome from Anadyr for refueling before commencing trade. Since the most lucrative portion of the trade occurred at the season's opening, the return to Nome worked hardship on operators of smaller vessels. Seattle traders with their large ships would be able to cream the trade. The Nome Chamber of Commerce made a counterproposal to the Russians that East Cape be designated the licensing center. If that were done, Nome traders would be on an equal footing with those of Seattle, because East Cape was just opposite Nome. Competition was hard enough under the previous conditions, with the well-established Swenson, Hibbard Company of Seattle doing a large share of the trade business, and the new restrictions could force Nome's mosquito fleet to the wall. To make the future even more threatening, the establishing of a new enterprise, well financed by Puget Sound business interests, was announced. The Siberian Company of Seattle planned to establish stores in Siberia, and it entered the field with an office in Nome and with two ships, the *Gedney* and the *Iskum*. The fact that outside businessmen were interested in Siberia despite existing competition proved that the field looked quite promising for the future.

The Russian Revolution provided an opportunity for Nome freebooters. Things did not settle down in Kamchatka and northeastern Siberia until 1922. Until then, chaotic conditions reigned, as small bands of Reds fought supporters of the czar for control of the region. Legitimate traders, among them Olaf Swenson of Seattle, suffered much disruption. But Swenson had the good reputation of an honest dealer who apparently did not traffic in booze, and he therefore gained permission to trade in Siberia until 1933. Each year, his ships called at coastal villages. The length of Swenson's tenure was remarkable, considering that even as famed and mighty a commercial enterprise as the Hudson's Bay Company was unable to establish itself in Kamchatka—and not for want of effort: the Hudson's Bay Company tried from 1921 to 1924 to establish stores before finally bowing to the vagaries of bureaucratic demands and withdrawing from the field.

But some of the Nome men also carried on through the 1920s, although, as the Communist government of Russia consolidated its authority, their days were numbered. The Bering Sea frontier became better policed and a Russian law of 1925 closed the stores of all foreigners except Swenson's. The hospitality Nome offered to White Russians who fled there to escape Red retribution did nothing to advance the town's business hopes.

During the revolution, Russians sometimes arrived unwillingly in Nome. Trader Johnny Fickel's schooner was arrested at Anadyr, and two Red customs officers were put aboard to oversee the unloading of the American's cargo. Fickel, a resourceful man, jumped the officers, tied them up, and steamed out of the harbor under cover of a thick fog. Once in Nome, Fickel graciously looked after the Russians until return transportation to Siberia was arranged for them.

Boosters of Alaska did not take kindly to the effects of the Russian Revolution on the peaceful pursuits of trading and mining. A leading article in the *Daily Alaska Dispatch* (Juneau) of June 1920 heralded a defeat suffered by "Bolsheviks" at the hands of Alaskan miners prospecting at Anadyr. According to the newspaper account, Americans had killed a dozen "bandits'' who had interfered with their work, had pillaged a Swenson store, and had threatened lives. An American cruiser should be sent to help the miners escape arrest, cried the *Dispatch:* "The unpaid interest on the U.S. loan to Russia was ample reason to send boats to protect miners''; the Americans were "venturesome northerners who, unterrified by bolshevik rule, are now in the country." There was every reason to believe, argued the *Dispatch,* that the north coast of Siberia offered an unlimited field for gold prospecting, trapping, and fishing. "There is no reason why Yankee pioneers should not exploit and open the country.'' [2] Such statements did not show any concern for a neighboring country's national sovereignty, and the new Soviet regime could not tolerate such American arrogance.

Trans–Bering Strait trading was severely curtailed by the Soviet government in the 1920s. Whether commerce will ever revive between the Bering Sea neighbors is questionable and dependent upon political and economic developments. It is possible that the utilization of some Alaskan mineral resource desirable to the Soviets could spur a renewal of commerce. Meanwhile, it seems likely that the geographic proximity of the two continents will be ignored except in matters concerning national defense.

Alaskan importation of Siberian reindeer ranks among the important cultural ties across the strait. That venture developed into the most original commercial enterprise ever launched in Alaska. The first reindeer had been imported from Siberia and Norway in the hope that Alaska's Eskimos could become skilled herdsmen and maintain the animals for sustenance. Reindeer thrived in the new country, particularly on the Seward Peninsula. In 1913, G. J. Lomen of Nome, an attorney, and his sons, who operated several businesses on the Seward Peninsula, bought herds from Eskimo and Lapp owners and began to market reindeer meat.

Between 1916 and 1920, the volume of reindeer meat handled increased from 10,650 to 257,000 pounds. Sales reached a

2. *Daily Alaska Dispatch,* June 25, 1920.

peak between 1928 and 1930, when 30,000 reindeer carcasses were shipped from northwest Alaska to Seattle. The Lomens employed 579 Eskimos, who herded and butchered the animals, and moved them by lighter out to the company's own ships for the long voyage from the Seward Peninsula south.

Initially, reindeer meat was advertised as a gourmet food. For a time, the transcontinental railroads featured it in their dining cars, and some of the better restaurants in major cities offered reindeer cutlets and roasts to patrons. The Lomens worked hard to market their product. One Christmas season, they organized a Santa Claus campaign in which Santa and his reindeer appeared in several different cities after a much-publicized—and fictitious—journey overland all the way from Nome.

Cattle dealers of the states did not take kindly to the emerging reindeer-meat competition. They urged the railroads to give up serving reindeer meat in preference to beef. Railroads valued the cattle-shipping business and quickly took reindeer from the menu. That setback annoyed the Lomens, but they carried on, branching out from specialty cuts to tinned dog food.

An unending protest against the Lomens' ownership of animals that had been intended for natives forced the company out of business in 1939. Eskimos, missionaries, and others repeatedly called upon the government to prevent whites from exploiting the reindeer. At congressional hearings, the Lomens defended their business, boasted of the numbers of Eskimos they employed, and argued that they had created a market outside, which could also be tapped by native herd-owners. But the Lomens could not convince Congress of the merit of their cause. The government prohibited white ownership and bought the company's herds for the benefit of native herdsmen.

Native herd-owners lacked the ability to repeat the Lomens' success. Poor management, overgrazing, and the predations of wolves drastically reduced the reindeer herds. Today, Alaska has only about thirty thousand of the animals, seventeen thousand of which are owned by natives and the rest by the government. The amount of meat marketed is a tiny fraction of what the Lomens achieved during their peak years. It is unlikely that a viable reindeer-meat industry will develop in the future; more likely, the attractive beasts will continue to delight children by conveying Santa Claus, but they will not displace beef from American dinner tables.

The reindeer-meat industry has always been an unusual enterprise of modest scale, successful for a brief time under the Lomens' name. But other Alaskan resources, most notably the area's fisheries, have attracted investment from the early years of the American era on.

7

Teeming Seas and Abundant Forests

*T*HE first commercial fish canneries were established in Alaska in 1878. Within fifty years, after the decline of mining in the North, salmon fisheries had become the territory's major industry. Alaska's marine resources had drawn men to the North, even before the development of the salmon fishery. An abundance of cod attracted Americans to Alaskan waters in 1865. San Francisco-based fishermen took cod in the waters southwest of Kodiak Island, along the Alaskan Peninsula, and in the Bering Sea. The first fixed shore station was established in 1876 at Pirate Cove or Popof Island.

Pacific salmon included king salmon, or Chinook; red and pink salmon; silver, or coho; and chum. All are spawned in rivers and tributary lakes, find their way to the sea, then in time return upriver to their place of origin to spawn and die. The life cycle of salmon determined the practices of Alaska's salmon-fishing industry. After their sojourn at sea, varying from two to seven years depending upon the species, salmon make a summer run for their spawning grounds. Fishermen take them in traps, nets, or by other means, as they approach and ascend the rivers of their origin. Salmon are highly perishable, once taken from the water, and must be processed—dried, salted, frozen, or canned—soon after they are caught. Because of that characteristic and the distance of most fishing grounds from major markets, the great majority of Alaska's salmon catch has always been canned at shore facilities near the fishery.

To maintain the available stocks of salmon, an adequate number of the fish must return to their spawning grounds. If, because of overfishing, the escapement is small, the depletion of stocks is inevitable. In the early years of the industry, unrestricted competition among cannery operators was the rule. If a company established a cannery at a place where the run proved particularly prosperous, other operators were likely to set up canneries in the same area. Under such conditions, salmon escapement could only be minimal.

Some restrictions were imposed upon fishermen in 1889. Dams on rivers were prohibited, as was weekend fishing, and salmon could not be taken above tidewaters in any river less than five hundred feet wide. Enforcement funds were allotted in 1892, but the funds were scanty, making serious policing impossible.

Eliza Scidmore, a travel writer who visited Alaska in 1892, marveled at the rivalries of salmon packers. Along the Karluk River on the west coast of Kodiak Island, she discovered ten canneries, one of them represented as the largest in the world. Since the river was only ten miles long and a hundred to six-hundred feet wide, the escapement permitted by ten competing operators must have been scanty indeed. Karluk canneries packed two hundred thousand cases containing three million fish in 1890. Yet, Scidmore reported, they enjoyed such abundance without tax, license, or any form of government interference.

Government agents warned Congress about the depletion dangers each year in the annual fisheries reports. In 1897, an agent advised that the competition could lead to bloodshed and "this bitter rivalry . . . if allowed to continue, will eventually destroy the salmon." [1] The agent cited instances of companies damming streams to prevent the ascent of salmon and thus thwart rival operators located upstream of the dam.

1. Richard A. Cooley, *Politics and Conservation: The Decline of the Alaska Salmon* (New York: Harper and Row, 1963), p. 27.

Inspectors did not have government transportation; they had to rely upon the good will of cannery operators to give them free transportation to the places they were to inspect. The ridiculousness of the situation was not lost on the first U.S. Treasury officials charged with enforcement. One reported that an inspector felt "more-or-less like a humbug; and when he detects a sly smile of derision on the face of the person whom he is presumed to have somewhat under surveillance it is not calculated to puff him up with official self-importance." [2] How, he asked, could he consider himself an embodiment of law when he must look to possible lawbreakers for indispensable assistance in the performance of his duties?

An angry agent reported in 1901 on the "absolute impracticability of maintaining a close surveillance over a stretch of country embracing thousands of miles in extent, and supporting fifty-five canneries and a score of salteries . . . which are supplied from fisheries numbering perhaps four hundred or five hundred, and which are separated by distances of five to over a hundred miles from the central plant, by the utmost vigilance and untiring activity of two officials was so entirely obvious that no argument was needed to establish the assertion." [3]

Despite the frequent cry against the inadequacy of conservation measures, remedies did not meet the needs. As early as 1904, a biologist recommended the closure of specific areas, but the canneries lobbied successfully against such stern measures. The canning industry insisted that government could check the salmon decline by providing hatcheries rather then restrictions. Appropriations for hatcheries were subsequently set aside.

Private companies on the Karluk River had first attempted to maintain the salmon runs by starting a hatchery in 1891. Several others went into operation within a few years. Aquaculture seemed to many to be the means of protecting the salmon. In 1892, the U.S. Fish Commissioner recommended that the government support hatcheries in Alaska, although no one really knew how efficient they might be.

2. Cooley, *Politics and Conservation,* p. 73.

3. *Report on the Salmon Fisheries of Alaska, 1901,* by Howard M. Kutchin (Washington, D.C.: Government Printing Office, 1902), p. 17.

For a few years after 1900, a federal government regulation required canneries to establish hatcheries capable of returning to the sea four times as many salmon fry as the total of their year's catch of mature salmon. Few packers obeyed the regulation. In some cases, there was no suitable place for aquaculture where the cannery was located, and smaller operators could not afford the cost of a hatchery. Furthermore, it was extremely difficult to find knowledgeable technicians. After a few years, the hatchery regulation was suspended.

Faith in hatcheries remained high, however, and in 1905 the Bureau of Fisheries—established in 1903 as a part of the U.S. Department of Commerce—built and operated two hatcheries. From 1906 to 1920, the government spent $525,000 on these installations and gave $600,000 rebates to large canneries maintaining hatcheries. Such largess exceeded by many times governmental appropriations for policing the canneries and for scientific research of the salmon.

Packers believed that they could eliminate government regulation of the canneries if they maintained a vigorous salmon restoration program. Regulations were irksome, even when indifferently enforced. The organ of the salmon industry, *Pacific Fisherman,* often extolled aquaculture. A lead article in 1911 was entitled "Hatcheries Make Extermination of Salmon Impossible." The magazine ignored the fact that it had not been determined how many fry escaped their predators and survived to maturity. Hatchery men gave extravagant, optimistic estimates that were not, however, based on scientific data. In 1912, the *Pacific Fisherman* thundered at a critic who predicted that the salmon would go the way of the buffalo. The bulletin stated that one hundred eggs were being left on the spawning grounds for every mature salmon caught. That, too, was simply a wild, self-serving guess.

The canned-salmon industry boomed for many years. With Seattle as home base for the industry, Washington state congressmen protected its interests quite effectively. Starting in 1911, annual reports of the territorial governors of Alaska warned of the possible depletion of the fishery, but these pessimistic forecasts were ignored. Governors also protested that natives were having a hard time providing themselves with salmon and were not offered jobs in the canneries. Governor John F. Strong complained vigorously in his 1914 report to the U.S. Secretary of the Interior: "The waters of Alaska have been exploited . . . for many years . . . and large individual fortunes have been accumulated . . . At no time, however, have the exploiters contributed anything like an adequate return for the privileges they have enjoyed." [4] The exploiters had ignored conservation.

In 1916, Governor Strong asked the U.S. Bureau of Fisheries to describe the status of the salmon. The response was a flat assertion that there was no danger of depletion. Claims to the contrary came from tourists who were not so knowledgeable about the resource as "those in authority who are competent to pass upon the matter." Strong challenged the Bureau of Fisheries' optimism in his report and pointed out the obvious menace of ever-increasing numbers of traps and canneries. Alaskans, who had observed the situation, "from the most illiterate native to the trained fishing expert and scholarly observer" were aware of the serious depletion.[5]

Residents of the territory determined to achieve two objectives: the control of fisheries in their own waters and the prohibition of traps. For the most part, the expensive and efficient traps were owned by canneries—thus the traps became the symbol for all that was pernicious in the exploitation of the fisheries by Outsiders. Alaskans had a delegate in Congress to wage their battle, but the struggle was uphill. The packers were well organized and had several powerful voices in Washington.

Even in granting home rule and a territorial legislature to Alaska, Congress bowed to the Alaska packers and withheld the right of fishery regulation from the territory. The action was an unprecedented snub and caused the packers' trade journal to chortle with glee that "the government has simply given Alaska a toy legislature to play politics with." Packer lobbyists were assisted in their efforts by the federal Bureau of Fisheries, which did not care to lose its control over Alaskan waters to the

4. Cooley, *Politics and Conservation,* p. 93.
5. Cooley, *Politics and Conservation,* p. 95.

territory. Self-righteously, the bureau boasted of the "vast amount of practical and scientific knowledge" that had been gathered "by men of unusual training and experience." [6]

Some Alaskan fishermen reacted violently against the cozy support the bureau gave to the packers, particularly in regard to the general use of fish traps by the canneries. When the fight for the abolition of traps seemed hopeless in 1918, it became commonplace for "pirates" to rob the traps of their salmon. The salmon were then sold by the thieves to the canneries. Packers cried for federal protection, and the U.S. Navy sent gunboats and subchasers to the North. Despite that, the piracy went on, and shoot-outs between cannery guards and trap-robbers were not unknown.

Salmon sales declined, for various reasons, after World War I, and packers became conservation-minded for the first time. For years, packers had denied that there was any threat to the resource; but in 1920, industry leaders, in a panic over reduced sales, admitted that overfishing had been carried on too long. In the same mood of depression caused by the slump, the packers blamed their old partner, the Bureau of Fisheries, for the depleted state of the fisheries. Thanks to pressure brought about by the packers, the Commissioner of Fisheries resigned.

All the uproar led to the introduction of a number of bills in Congress, and in 1924 the White Act became law. The White Act was widely heralded as the means by which the federal government could rationally protect the fisheries. The government established escapement limits and gave the Bureau of Fisheries authority to arrest violators of the new restrictions on the equipment, as well as fishermen caught in reserved areas or fishing outside the established season. Packers lost their interest in conservation as soon as the act was passed because the market conditions that had stimulated conservation sentiment altered radically. Suddenly there was a great demand for salmon, and the salmon pack in 1924 exceeded all those of the past with the exception of the two peak war years. Bureau of Fisheries and packers forgot all fears of the depletion of the resource, and the

6. Cooley, *Politics and Conservation*, p. 96.

salmon pack of the next several years reflected the steady market demand. Of course, from time to time, the packers praised the regulations of the White Act and insisted that their large take gave evidence of the wisdom of its measures. In fact, however, their overfishing was in obvious disregard of the future prospects of the fisheries and imperiled their existence.

Alaska's congressional delegates in the 1920s and 1930s, Dan Sutherland and Anthony J. Dimond, were no match for the packer lobbyists whenever the delegates renewed their protests against fish traps and called for some protection of the interests of resident Alaskan fishermen. Congress heeded the arguments of the major packers and accepted their assurances that all was well with the fishery and with the Alaskan fishermen.

Government policies did not really change until 1933, when the Bureau of Fisheries took a hard look at the salmon-catch statistics. Figures showed an obvious depletion that hatcheries had not been able to check. The commissioner then closed down the two remaining government hatcheries and deplored what he called a complete waste of public funds over the years of hatchery support.

The first major success gained by the territory against the opposition of the salmon lobby came after World War II, when Governor Ernest Gruening finally succeeded in imposing new taxes on the packers. Gruening's struggle for revenue is described elsewhere. Taxation did not halt the course of the depletion of the fisheries, however. By 1953, the total pack was less than three million cases—the second lowest in forty-two years. It was impossible for anyone to ignore the crisis that had been created by overfishing. To complicate the situation further and to provide another threat to the fisheries, Japanese fleets began fishing off Alaska in the mid-1950s, as they had before World War II. Packers tried to make the Japanese the scapegoats of the salmon depletion but, as economist Richard Cooley noted, the downward trend in salmon harvests had begun almost two decades before the Japanese started fishing on the high seas.

Admission to statehood of Alaska in 1959 resulted at last in the transfer of fishery regulation within Alaskan waters to the new state. Responsibility for international regulation of the high-seas fisheries remained with the federal government, and negotiations with foreign governments have proved to be interminable exercises. But the transfer of authority to the state did not end the threat to the fisheries. In 1963, Cooley warned that "unless the state is willing to embark upon a long-range program based on a complete reformulation of the conservation problem in terms of economic, political, social, and biological reality," Alaska would do no better than the federal government had done.[7] Successive state administrations have insisted that Alaska has developed an effective program; and yet, in 1976, the future prosperity of the fisheries looks very gloomy. Alaskans no longer blame greedy packers and indifferent federal agencies for the crisis, but it appears that many years' overfishing, together with recent fishing in international waters by fleets of several nations, has produced an irremediable situation.

Currently, the interest in salmon aquaculture is growing in Alaska. Several hatcheries, operating as nonprofit corporations, are attempting to reverse the trend of salmon depletion. Considerably more is known about salmon and their natural environment today than was known earlier, and those involved are confident of the eventual success of aquaculture.

The quest for an economic base in fisheries has long been frustrating for Alaskans. Similarly, hopes for timber production have not been fulfilled, although the pattern of development has varied greatly between the two resources.

Early boosters of Alaska did not overlook the potential value of its timber. A voyage along the Inside Passage of southeastern Alaska was in itself enough to evoke grandiose speculations on the wealth represented by the towering forests of western hemlock, Sitka spruce, and western red cedar that stretched as far as the eye could see. Here was a visible resource requiring no prospecting: just build a pulp mill and go to work. The trees grew thickly from tidewater to timberline, furnishing many millions of board feet, enough to sustain an industry on a perpetual-yield basis. But gleeful cries and prideful pointing did not create a pulp industry. The history of logging in Alaska resembles that of agriculture. The clamor over the resource and its develop-

7. Cooley, *Politics and Conservation*, p. 205.

ment has echoed more robustly than the lumberjack's axe.

Genuine interest in producing pulp in Alaska did not arise until about 1914. Prior to that time, the forests of the West produced all that was needed and Alaskan timber was too distant for practical consideration. All that changed with the tremendous demands for paper that grew out of World War I. Paper makers called upon the government for a survey of all federal lands to ascertain the quantity of timber available. Alaska was to be included in the survey. Canada provided most of the pulp needs of the United States at that time, and industry leaders argued that the U.S. should not remain dependent on another nation when Alaska's forests were so prolific.

Government officials shared the concern of industry for the production of pulp in Alaska. In 1920, Secretary of Agriculture Edwin T. Meredith promoted the notion vigorously: "The government owes it to Alaska to develop its resources and foster its economic growth," he wrote. "The opening up of the forests of Alaska for the development of the paper industry will supply one of the most critical needs of the United States." An industrial journal voiced the same sentiments: "The time seems to be ripe for the extensive exploitation of Alaskan pulpwood." [8] Other experts predicted that two or possibly three pulp mills would be in operation in Alaska by 1924.

One small mill was put into operation at Speel River near Juneau in 1922 and began producing twenty tons of pulp daily. The pulp was shipped to California and praised as a superior product. Production and shipping proved too expensive, however, and after a couple of years the mill folded. Economic realities dimmed the dreams of promoters—but only temporarily. Whenever the supply of paper seemed to be waning, either the U.S. Forest Service or industry leaders would issue a clarion call for the development of an Alaskan product. Pessimists countered with warnings that transport costs and a lack of water power were handicaps not to be overcome—and nothing was done.

Interest in Alaska revived after World War II. A pulp mill built at Ketchikan in 1952 and 1953 went into production in

8. David D. Smith, "Pulp, Paper, and Alaska," *Pacific Northwest Quarterly*, April 1975, p. 63.

1954. The long-held dream materialized, and the mill, which employed nine hundred workers, was expanded in 1956.

The opening of the Ketchikan mill in 1954 was an event of magnitude. Territorial Governor B. Frank Heintzleman heralded the mill as the solution to Alaska's economic woes: "For Alaskans, the project marks the first realization of a dream and years of effort to get a major industry started in the vast, untapped virgin forests of the Territory's southeastern reaches." [9] The newly created pulp industry planned to build other mills at Juneau and elsewhere, increasing the chances to beat unemployment on the Panhandle.

But the growth in pulp production did not keep pace with the governor's expectations. Japanese interests began building a timber mill at Sitka in 1954, after the United States government restricted the export of round logs and prohibited the employment of Japanese woodcutters. Some lumber was shipped to Japan from southeastern Alaska in 1955, and construction of a pulp mill began in 1956. By January 1960, the mill was shipping 340 tons of bleached pulp per day.

A third mill, planned by U.S. Plywood-Champion Papers, Incorporated, after contracting for 8.75 billion board feet from the Tongass National Forest, was held up by the courts in 1968 because of the opposition of conservationists, and the project was cancelled in 1976. A district court ruling against clear-cutting in January 1976 has clouded prospects even more. Unless the adverse decision is overturned, the pulp industry may close down in Alaska because of the high costs of selective cutting.

Although the development of the salmon fisheries and the timber resources of Alaska have each followed a distinct pattern, they held some basic characteristics in common. Government regulations are a predominant factor in the utilization of both resources; and outside investors have had to exploit these resources because of the high costs of producing a yield. By now, these are familiar themes. But what of the greatest resource of all—the land itself? Surely the failure of agricultural production has been the foremost stumbling block in the path of Alaska's economic development.

9. Smith, "Pulp, Paper, and Alaska," p. 68.

8

Tyranny of Climate
and Distances

$\mathcal{O}\!\mathcal{S}$UCH greenery as delights and refreshes the eye, white-crowned mountains towering in the distance, rivers and lakes glistening in the sunshine—the vastness and promise of the land was almost too much to take in. The pristine Tanana valley was a scene so magnificent that it induced level-headed men to turn prophets. So it was with Judge James Wickersham, a man whose profession called for a judicial temperament; he was moved to declaim that the valley would one day become the breadbasket of Alaska—that its soil would support a million people. At the time he made that observation, in 1903, the soil of the valley had never been tilled. Its virgin expanse promised limitless potential to a visionary like Wickersham, who looked beyond the elusive glitter of gold placers to the more conventional wealth of the land.

Other men followed in the judge's footsteps, making similar predictions that the Tanana valley would surely flourish one day. Equal agricultural promise has been held out for other parts of Alaska, most notably Kodiak Island and the Matanuska Valley. Few books on Alaska published in the last seventy years have been without photographs of outsized cabbages and prodigious strawberries. After all, as Wickersham pointed out, the interior of Alaska, with its high altitude, gets more sunshine during the summer than California does during the same months. The promise of abundance has been offered with as much persistence as the opposite representation of a land of desolation, a frigid place of eternal snow and ice.

A cooler view than Wickersham's had been expressed earlier by the great scientist William Healy Dall. Dall had been a member of the Western Union Telegraph Expedition from 1865 to 1867 and in subsequent years had continued to carry on his scientific work in the North. By 1895, Dall had seen great changes: "The whaling and sealing industries . . . are practically exhausted, the fur trade is in its decadence, the salmon canning in the full tide of prosperity, but conducted in a wasteful and destructive manner which cannot long be continued with impunity." Not that Alaska's resources were being dried up generally: "The cod and herring fisheries are imperfectly developed, but have a substantial future with proper treatment. Mineral resources and timber have hardly been touched." [1]

After thirty years of intimate acquaintance with the North, Dall could forecast its prospects with some authority. He was a scientist without an axe to grind, neither booster nor conservationist. As the nineteenth century drew to a close, Alaska seemed to Dall to be in a state of transition: "The industries of the unexploited wilderness are passing away, while the time of steady, businesslike development of the more latent resources has not yet arrived." Clearly, the region had another value similar to that of Norway as the goal of tourists, hunters, and fishermen who would voyage north to enjoy the magnificent scenery—the glaciers, volcanoes, and other natural splendors. On agricultural prospects, Dall's opinion was somewhat conservative and quite sound: agriculture would be restricted to "gardening and the culture of quick-growing and hardy vegetables for local use." In looking to the long-run potential of Alaska, the scientist was cautiously optimistic. There would be frequent "failures and disappointments" in the development of most Alaskan industries, he guessed, because "untrained hands" would be called upon for the work, "but when the pressure of

1. Dall, "Alaska as It Was and Is," p. 147.

population enforces more sensible methods the territory will support in reasonable comfort a fair number of hardy and industrious inhabitants." [2]

Prophets have always flourished in Alaska. There is so much space for speculation, so much contrast and variety to inflame the imagination. Those who supported Seward's purchase of Alaska came forward with all kinds of optimistic arguments concerning the resource riches of the region. Little was known of the true potential, but that did not matter. It was easy enough to launch visionary balloons in the absence of knowledge.

But Alaskans themselves clashed on the resource potential of the region, just as they did on the question of home rule. As might be suspected, those favoring home rule—in the manner of Wickersham envisioning the prodigious potential wheat fields of the Tanana valley—tended to call for speedy development of natural resources. Such optimists as Wickersham met the opposition of anti-home-rulers like Wilds P. Richardson, Alaska's road commissioner, who did not believe in the farming potential and who believed that caution and conservation were the best courses to follow.

The years of high mineral yield let people forget their debate over Alaska's economic potential, temporarily. As the production of minerals slowed down, each side took up its cause again. Writing in 1928, Richardson argued that Americans had been deceived into believing that the purchase of Alaska was a great business bargain. Why boast of the purchase price of only $7.2 million when the government had spent another $200 million on the territory, including $70 million for a railroad to aid economic development, asked Richardson. It amused him that "an Alaskan enthusiast, speaking before a committee of Congress, declared the territory to be the richest possession under the American flag and the cheapest piece of real estate since a certain mythical transaction in Biblical times." [3]

That was nonsense, according to Richardson, who felt that "after sixty years of ownership, assertions about the territory should be supported by a substantial showing of developed re-

2. Dall, "Alaska as It Was and Is," p. 148.
3. Wilds P. Richardson, "Alaska," *Harper's*, March 1928, p. 111.

sources, wealth, and population." Those who predicted a great rush of new residents with the building of the Seward-Fairbanks railroad were disappointed. For a better example of a land bargain, Richardson suggested that the Louisiana Purchase be considered. "In 1920 the little state of Iowa alone produced, in the value of her farm products, more than the total output of Alaska from all sources from the date of its purchase up to that time, while the state of Louisiana produced furs last year . . . worth five times the value of the furs exported from Alaska in the same year." [4]

Richardson professed to believe that the exaggeration of Alaska's wealth would hurt the territory's development. At hearings conducted in 1914, he had opposed the plan to build the Alaska Railroad and, of course, delegate James Wicker-sham, among other Alaskans, had favored construction. Richardson resented the railroad because he wanted the government to spend more on trails and roads—which were the transport links he managed.

Richardson pointed out that much of the enthusiasm for Alaskan development came from Seattle. The close relationship between Seattle business interests and Alaska had existed since the Klondike gold rush. At times, members of Congress representing Washington State helped greatly to support causes favored by Alaska's delegate; at other times they opposed Alaska's representative. It was just a matter of what seemed most beneficial to Seattle.

Congress first appropriated money for the investigation of Alaska's agricultural potential in 1898. The five-thousand-dollar investigation resulted in a favorable report recommending that the federal government establish agricultural experiment stations in Alaska. Over the next five years, such stations were established at Sitka, Kenai, Copper Center, Kodiak, and Rampart. Several stations closed down after a few years, but experiments continued at research stations at Fairbanks and in the Matanuska Valley. The program operated on a very limited budget, but it accomplished important research on soils, costs, and the most suitable kinds of crops.

4. Richardson, "Alaska," p. 111.

Agricultural experts brimmed with enthusiasm for production prospects in Alaska. From 1916 to 1941, seven revisions of a bulletin providing *Information for Prospective Settlers in Alaska* were published by the U.S. Department of Agriculture. Each of these publications stated that an estimated one hundred thousand square miles of land suitable for tilling and grazing existed in Alaska: "The agricultural area is, therefore, as large as the combined ares of the states of Pennsylvania, Maryland, Delaware, New Jersey, Connecticut, Massachusetts, Vermont, and New Hampshire; and it should be capable of supporting a population nearly equal to that supported by the agricultural products of those states." [5] The bulletin admitted to uncertainties, however. Much of Alaska's soil was poor; brown bears menaced sheep and cattle, and freight costs could be heavy; despite such reservations, however, the bulletin urged readers to take up a homestead.

But few settlers cared to venture into agriculture. Too many handicaps existed. The tyranny of long distances and high freight costs limited production to a marginal level. A paucity of roads, a small population and, hence, a very limited market and a lack of capital contributed considerably to hampering the growth of the industry. The climate also presented a serious obstacle. Devastating frosts have occurred repeatedly in the Tanana Valley in August. Furthermore, the soil there and elsewhere in the territory lacked nutrients. Expensive fertilizers added heavily to the costs of production. Finally, farmers in Alaska suffered from outside competition. Invariably, goods shipped in from Seattle sold for less than local products. Something had to be done to alleviate such problems, insisted many Alaskans. In response to their plea, and to ease the effects of the depression, the federal government undertook the bold effort of sponsoring an agricultural colony in Alaska.

In the spring of 1935, a small army of carpenters and 202 colonists from the Midwest invaded Alaska's Matanuska Valley. They had come to create a Garden of Eden in the wilderness, or at least to make the valley bloom. Funded by New Deal legisla-

---

5. C. C. Georgeson, *Information for Prospective Settlers in Alaska* (Washington, D.C.: Government Printing Office, 1916), p. 9.

tion, the Alaskan colony was just a small part of a relocation of families within the United States. Rural poverty, widespread unemployment, and faith in land settlement motivated the program that resulted in the Matanuska colony and others. Much publicity attended the effort in Alaska because the agricultural experiment conflicted so sharply with the popular image of the region's climate. But for Alaskans and boosters of Alaska, the colony had a larger meaning. Here, at last, they argued, the federal government was substantially investing in the agricultural potential of the territory. Once the rugged, experienced colonizers had demonstrated that farming could be conducted successfully on a large scale in Alaska, others would take their chances on the North. The prophecies of Judge James Wickersham and others who had boasted of Alaska's future bounty would be fulfilled.

The Matanuska Valley is beautiful. Situated about fifty miles north of Anchorage, it is surrounded by lofty mountains on three sides. On the fourth side, it opens to Knik Arm, a part of Cook Inlet that pierces into the interior some two hundred miles from the main body of the North Pacific. But a spectacular setting is not enough; much work had to be done to make the land thrive.

Planners of the colony felt confident that it would prosper. Some nine thousand people lived along the rail belt; thus an assured market existed. Hardy vegetables and grain would grow well in the valley. Land was cheap or free, and timber for building was readily available. The new community would spark the territory's economic development. And the settlers, who faced starvation in the South, would emerge as prosperous farmers.

Seven press associations and a newsreel company sent representatives north with the colonists to report on the experiment. Hundreds of news stories heralded the colony as a reminder that the last wilderness in North America still existed and observed proudly that American frontiersmen dared to challenge it. *Time* magazine romanced on the safety-valve feature of the migration: "Many an observer has pointed out that past U.S. depressions were relieved by mass migration to the frontier, that the present depression is uniquely acute because that safety-valve is gone."

But hope remained because "there is one last U.S. frontier: Alaska." [6]

Except for a survey of forty-acre lots, no advance work was done prior to the arrival of the farmers at Palmer, the site of the Matanuska Valley experiment. Families lived in tents and assisted the six hundred carpenters who were sent north to build houses. To some arrivals, the odds-on success seemed far too formidable. The weather was not promising, either. Everyone assured the discouraged pioneers that it never rained in the spring, although the late summer was blessed with a nice rainfall. Yet in May and June of 1935, rain poured in never-ending sheets. All was mud and chaos in the Matanuska, and a number of fed-up farmers demanded passage money to go back home to the Midwest, where a man had a chance against the elements. Those who remained discovered that Alaska was cold and windy, that forty-acre tracts were too small to sustain a family, that drainage was a serious problem, that the soil was not uniformly good, that the kinds of crops they were accustomed to raising were not suited to the valley, that shipping costs prohibited the service of any but the small local market of Anchorage, and that it was not pleasant to have one's life directed by a federal bureaucracy.

The colony stumbled along for five years of discord and hard scrabbling until the establishment of a huge military base at Fort Richardson in 1940 provided a market. Most colonizers found it more profitable to work at defense jobs, however, and, if they farmed at all, it was a part-time effort. After World War II, the decline continued, and today there is little farming in the valley. Anchorage's booming population growth has made it more profitable to subdivide farm tracts for residential lots than to produce food.

In retrospect, the Matanuska colony planting appears ridiculous. Certainly an effort to increase Alaska's population slightly could not be ranked very highly on a list of depression relief measures. Critics of the colony pointed out that, for an investment no larger than it took to place a settler in Alaska, a good

6. *Time*, May 6, 1935, p. 17.

Iowa farm—a working farm—could have been purchased by the government. The project had been dreamed up by social workers who wanted to recover America's pioneer past. It was the romantic notion of our heritage that attracted the enthusiasm of the *New York Times* and other newspapers. In the grip of such nostalgic longings and the exoticism of Alaska, no one cared to look coldly at the practicalities of the resettlement.

The failure of the colony is only one chapter of Alaska's agricultural history, but it is significant. For once, the government answered the pleas of Alaskans for agricultural development and carried through a sizable project; and, even if original expectations were not met, the town of Palmer was created and still exists. But even with such help, the tyrannies of distance, climate, and other obstacles proved too formidable. Boosters of Alaska's agricultural future still exist. A combination of events—population growth, new technology, and rising freight rates—might yet alter the situation. It is not easy to imagine such a change, however, as a review of Alaska's farming history does not encourage optimism.

The Matanuska experiment failed to provide a solution to one of Alaska's perennial economic problems, but at least that government enterprise pleased most Alaskans. Other government interventions caused great resentment. Creation of national forests and restrictions on resource utilization irked residents on several occasions—particularly the withdrawal of coal lands from public entry during the Progressive era.

9

Enemies of Alaska's Progress

$\mathcal{A}$GRICULTURE in Alaska faltered because of transport costs and climate. Alaskans have generally recognized that nature, rather than some conspiracy hatched in Washington, D.C., or Seattle, must be blamed for the area's limited food production. But northerners certainly complained about high costs and limited commercial development when these were dictated by government policies. Both the coal lands dispute and the ceaseless appeals for lower freight rates exemplify traditional Alaskan attitudes. Urging the government to remove restrictions on land use while calling for regulation of shipping may be inconsistent—but supporters of those demands did not think so.

The coal lands dispute arose out of the Progressive reform movement that enlivened the national political scene in the early years of this century. Among the tenets of Progressives was the conviction that the urbanization and industrialization of America had enriched a few at the expense of many: Why, they asked, should public lands be given to railroads, which then charged excessive freight rates? Many resources that should have been developed for the good of all were in fact controlled by corporate interests. The growing national tendency toward monopolistic power had to be checked if living conditions were to improve.

Alaskans had been concerned about monopolies as well, particularly the Morgan-Guggenheim syndicate that had invested

97

heavily in gold-mining properties all over the territory, developed the fabulously rich copper lode near Chitina, and dominated maritime shipping. But most Alaskans did not appreciate other thrusts of the Progressive reformers, especially that concerning the use of natural resources. Alaskans were dismayed at the creation of the Tongass and Chugach national forests in 1904 and 1907. These forests included practically all of southeastern Alaska, where much of the population lived, as well as the coastal region surrounding Prince William Sound.

But even more shocking to Alaskans was the executive order issued by President Theodore Roosevelt in 1906, which prohibited coal mining on the public domain. Such stunning and widespread restrictions of land use seemed to doom the hopes of miners and potential homesteaders. Gold mining was declining but enthusiastic boosters predicted a great future for coal production. They complained that, since all of Alaska's widely dispersed coal lands lay within public domain, Roosevelt's decree effectively locked up the resource.

Alaskans believed open land was the key to their economic well-being and hoped for more residents. But a general decline in mining, for copper and silver as well as gold, hurt Alaska more than the withdrawal of coal lands. The population decreased from 64,356 in 1910 to only 55,036 in 1920. Mining declined because of a shortage of men and capital during World War I and the closure of the great Treadwell gold mine at Juneau because of a flood during the same period.

Gifford Pinchot, Chief Forester of the United States, had influenced Roosevelt to close public entry to all coal lands in Alaska. Pinchot believed that a block of coal land known as the Cunningham claims were being held surreptitiously for the Morgan-Guggenheim syndicate. If the syndicate gained control of these claims, it could squeeze other operators out of business with the help of its already dominant shipping operation.

Secretary of Interior Richard Ballinger favored the development of the Cunningham claims and opposed Pinchot. The ensuing public squabble over Ballinger's motivations and the soundness of Pinchot's views helped to create a schism within the Republican party. Roosevelt campaigned unsuccessfully against William Howard Taft in 1912 as a third-party candidate. The land-use issue was intimately related to Alaskans' hopes for self-government. Until the people of the territory had some voice in the potential process, they cried, policies would be determined by distant, ignorant federal bureaucrats. Land use would be frozen and development would be forever retarded. "Every one with good sense," wrote one journalist, "will see that resident Alaskans committed to their country's welfare naturally understand the needs of the north much better than the best informed foreigner." It was only fair to allow Alaskans the right to manage their own affairs. "The greatest obstacle to the progress of Alaska and the growth of her population is the persistent refusal of the United States government to allow the citizens of the Northland to use the abounding resources of the country for the building up of a national life on the lines so successfully followed by English-speaking colonists for centuries." The tried-and-true methods "which have won the wilderness to civilization are to be abandoned." [1]

Alaskans were not complacent in their resistance to what they termed "communism and other crank schemes" that they thought the federal government foisted upon them. Sometimes their language of protest was harsh and even a little exaggerated. Writing in the *Alaska-Yukon Magazine* in 1912, journalist George E. Baldwin summarized the history of the territory from 1867. Until the withdrawal of coal lands by President Theodore Roosevelt in 1906, there had not been any indication that Alaskans would be denied the "'same just and generous treatment" granted to other pioneers. What had happened to change this? Baldwin reasoned that "suddenly there arose a school of political economists that found out that everything done in the past had been wrong; that our statesmen had been fools or knaves, or both; that our pioneers had been vandals and thieves." A bunch of theorizing cranks had started an unequaled campaign of venom and deliberate lying. "The present inhabitants and their rights were to be disregarded, the resources of Alaska managed

---

1. L. Eby, "The Cunningham Story of Ethics of Coal Situation in Alaska," *Alaska-Yukon Magazine*, March 1912, pp. 354–355.

as an estate," the government debt was to be liquidated, and huge pensions were to be paid to all Americans out of Alaska's resources. According to Baldwin, the "crazy communists" were not the real leaders of this movement but rather federal bureaucrats anxious to exercise despotic control, "depriving the people of their land heritage and placing on their necks the iron collar of serfdom." [2]

Baldwin decried the doctrines of Gifford Pinchot: "When the high priest of conservation, the prince of shadow dancers, recently visited Alaska to gloat over his handiwork of empty houses, deserted villages, dying towns, arrested development, bankrupt pioneers, and the blasted hopes of sturdy, self-reliant American citizens, it is striking comment on the law-abiding character of our people that he came back at all." [3]

Baldwin's assessment of the position of "doctrinaire conservationists" was striking: they would attempt to undo all that our ancestors had done to subdue the wilderness and populate it with "the freest and most intelligent people on the face of the earth." To have that record sullied by the "monumental folly" of the creation of the vast forest reserves of Alaska was too awful! If one wished to see in the world the practice of the doctrinaire conservationists carried to its logical conclusion, it was possible to do so: "In equatorial Africa live one hundred and sixty million graduate Ethiopian conservationists" whose resources have not changed since Caesar's time. "These people live in one grand forest reserve . . . their contributions to civilization and progress have been those twin blessings, slavery and cannibalism." The analogy was clear to Baldwin. The benighted Africans were conserving their resources. Each and every one of "these Senegambian gentlemen is entitled to receive from Gifford's correspondence school the degree of Doctor of Conservation." [4]

Alaskans should have the same right of untrammeled development accorded to other territories, he argued. "This lock-up,

2. George E. Baldwin, "Conservative Faddists Arrest Progress and Seek to Supplant Self-Government with Bureaucracy," *Alaska-Yukon Magazine,* February 1912, p. 44.

3. Baldwin, "Conservative Faddists," p. 44.

4. Baldwin, "Conservative Faddists," p. 44.

tie-up, bottle-up communistic policy has gone far enough.'' Individual initiative and enterprise had made the nation great; keep ''communist experiments'' out of Alaska! [5]

As president, Theodore Roosevelt had hoped that Congress would pass new legislation to permit the mining of coal and other minerals in Alaska and forestall monopolistic control. Congress, however, moved slowly in dealing with land matters and the railroad construction so critical to Alaskan hopes. In 1910, the U.S. Geological Survey head in Alaska, Alfred H. Brooks, set forth the relationship: ''As in previous years, the lack of cheap fuel is the greatest hindrance to the advancement of the mining industry in Alaska.'' [6] No one would finance a railroad that had to operate on expensive, imported fuel.

Residents of Cordova grew particularly restive over the coal situation. They resolved to make a forceful protest and banded together under their civic leaders, among them Mayor Austin Lathrop. Three hundred strong, the irate men marched to the dock where British Columbia coal had been unloaded. With great zest, the men shoveled some of the coal into the bay. The performance was in deliberate emulation of the Boston Tea Party of revolutionary times, and it did gain some national attention. Newspapers of Seattle, San Francisco, Philadelphia, and other cities applauded the self-help of the Cordovans and called on the government to settle the coal-lands problem—but to no immediate effect.

In Katalla, Pinchot was burned in effigy and a proclamation was posted:

> PINCHOT, MY POLICY
> No patents to coal lands!
> All timber in forest reserves!
> Bottle up Alaska!
> Save Alaska for all time to come! [7]

The language of the proclamation has a familiar ring for anyone who followed the more recent controversy over the Alaska

5. Baldwin, ''Conservative Faddists,'' p. 44.
6. Gruening, *State of Alaska*, p. 132.
7. Gruening, *State of Alaska*, p. 135.

oil pipeline. As in the coal dispute, the proponents of development felt that they were being sacrificed to conservation hysteria. Once again, they argued, Alaskans were being denied economic opportunity by those who wished to "save Alaska for all time to come."

In 1914, Congress passed a law that provided for the leasing of coal lands in Alaska. Leases could be obtained by both industry and the public. There was no great rush of investors, although the government mined coal in the Matanuska Valley in anticipation of the Alaska Railroad, which was then under construction. In the early 1920s, one private mining operation finally opened in the Nenana coal fields along the route of the railroad. That mine still produces coal for the city of Fairbanks, but coal is not exported from Alaska. Ernest Gruening has argued that a profitable export industry would have developed in coal but for the delay caused by the government's withdrawal of public lands. During the withdrawal period—1906 to 1914—the opening of the Panama Canal lowered coal freight rates from the east to the west coasts, and California's petroleum production rose. If Alaska's coal could have been exported earlier, Gruening stated, those events could not have affected the territory's coal industry. Gruening's arguments seem somewhat tenuous, considering that costs of transport from Alaska have always been high. It has never been economically feasible to ship any but valuable minerals—gold and copper, for the most part—for consumption elsewhere.

But Alaskans have been much more concerned about incoming freight from Seattle than in the southbound rates and have been complaining about the northbound rates since 1867. Until World War II, ships brought all Outside products to northern residents and still bring most of them. Before government regulation, rates seemed excessive to those dependent upon the shippers—and conditions did not seem to improve much when rates were fixed by the government. Shipping companies could raise numerous, irrefutable arguments on their high costs because of long distances, the many small ports requiring service, the short season beyond the Aleutians, seasonable economic activity, and one-way cargoes.

Regular monthly shipping service to Alaska began in 1869 and developed rapidly. In the 1870s, the Pacific Coast Steamship Company operated fourteen ships and virtually monopolized the trade. During the Klondike gold rush, Seattle replaced San Francisco as the main home port for shippers of Alaskan freight and passengers, and the Seattle-based Alaska Steamship Company and the Pacific Steamship Company vied for dominance in Alaska shipping, with perhaps forty other, smaller companies that came and went between the Klondike rush and World War II. The Pacific Steamship Company withdrew from the Alaska trade early in the 1930s, but by then a new firm, Northland Transportation Company, was challenging Alaska Steamship Company and eventually purchased controlling interest in Alaska Steam.

The importance of Seattle as the hub of communications for Alaska can not be overstressed. Until recently, the telegraph system was maintained by the U.S. Army Alaska Communication System, which was headquartered in Seattle. Most of the food that Alaskans eat, much of their clothing, most building materials, equipment, and everything else that Alaskans use—85 percent of all materials consumed—all are shipped in from the port of Seattle. Only a minimal portion of freighting is shipped over the Alaska Highway, because sea-route costs are lower. Cargo bound for the interior must be transferred to trucks or railroad cars at Anchorage but, except for Fairbanks, almost all Alaskan towns of any importance can be reached directly by sea.

Because Seattle is the center of distribution for Alaska, certain anomolies exist. Fish caught on Cook Inlet is not marketed directly in Anchorage; nor are the salmon of Panhandle waters or Bristol Bay shipped from there to Anchorage or Fairbanks. Instead, sea products are sent to Seattle where, eventually, they can be shipped north to fill Alaskan orders. Freight rates and the lack of a marketing system in Alaska make such a circuitous transport system cheaper than any other, thus far.

Freight rates rose in Alaska from 1915 onward until the late 1940s. To gain some relief from that situation, the territorial legislature established the Alaska Territorial Shipping Board in

1919 and gave that body an appropriation of $300,000, authorizing it to go into the steamship freight-and-passenger business if that appeared to be called for. A study indicated that some form of subsidy was necessary, because the scattered, small ports in Alaska needed service. An annual tax of three dollars per net ton on all ships calling at Alaska ports was proposed. The proceeds of the tax were to be used by the board to subsidize remote ports. Nothing came of the plan, however, and the board went out of existence.

In 1940, an official investigation was undertaken when the principal carriers asked for a 50 percent tariff increase. Extensive hearings were held in Seattle, Ketchikan, Juneau, and Anchorage. The carriers were well represented, but their customers, who usually passed on freight charges to consumers, anyway, were reluctant to appear and testify.

In August of 1941, the Maritime Commission found that the current rates were not too high, under the circumstances. Conditions changed rapidly when World War II started. War-time cargo insurance rates increased drastically, and the government ordered a 48 percent hazard bonus paid to all crew members in Alaskan waters. The carriers asked for and immediately received permission from the Maritime Commission to put a surcharge of 45 percent on all Alaska freight rates and passenger fares. Alaskans protested violently, and the investigation of 1940 was reopened. The federal government agreed to pay the extra costs; otherwise, the Alaskan cost of living would have gone up immediately by one third. In March of 1942, the Maritime Commission ordered the surcharge cut to 20 percent for southeastern Alaskan ports, but did permit it to remain at the 45 percent rate for the rest of Alaska. Subsequently, the latter surcharge was reduced to 25 percent.

The War Shipping Administration requisitioned the entire Alaskan fleet in 1942. The ships were assigned back to the carrier companies, who operated them as agents of the government. These were profitable years—and no one complained.

The rate situation did not improve until the 1960s with the introduction of containerized cargo on faster and more economical ships. The build-up of the resident population created a heavier demand for goods, but the rivalry of trucking companies has helped to keep the tariffs at a reasonable level.

Sore points remain, however, such as the Jones Act. The Jones Act of 1920 was intended to foster the nation's merchant marine by banning the service of foreign vessels between two American ports. Alaskans considered that discriminatory against them because of their dependence upon sea transport; they have held that competition offered by foreign shippers could reduce the freight rates on Alaska-bound cargoes.

Some Alaskans have contended that the federal government should directly subsidize marine shipping to Alaska. Such a subsidy would reward northern residents for keeping watch over the region's resources until national needs compelled their exploitation. That view contains a certain logic. Gold extraction was expedited because a resident population provided some manpower and services; and the military build-up of World War II moved swiftly because communities and a local labor force existed.

But it could also be argued effectively that the federal government has always subsidized Alaskans heavily—and particularly since World War II created the need to defend the territory. Defense spending during and after the war shifted the economic base from the private to the public sector and stimulated a rapid growth.

10

Spending for Defense

N June 1942, Japanese forces landed on Kiska and Attu in the Aleutian Islands and attacked the American military base at Dutch Harbor. The campaign following that invasion was notable for being the only one in World War II fought in North America as well as for the bizarre nature of some of its incidents. In retrospect, the entire performance could be seen as an exercise in inanity except for the tragic fact that a half-million men suffered in the fog-bound North Pacific and thousands laid down their lives there.

In September 1939, after Hitler's panzer divisions crunched into Poland, U.S. military planners began studying maps of Alaska. Their survey did not take long: the military presence in the North at that time consisted of a three-hundred-man garrison at Chilkoot Barracks near Haines. Even the Aleutians lacked defenses, despite the strategic importance of their position stretching across the North Pacific as potential stepping stones to Asia. As a provision of the Naval Disarmament Treaty of 1922, the United States had agreed not to fortify the islands. In 1934, Japan renounced the treaty, but the United States did nothing to strengthen the northern defensive perimeter until World War II broke out in Europe. Then, particularly after Pearl Harbor, the U.S. hurriedly remedied the oversight. Construction projects abounded all over the territory as airfields and military bases were created. Military expenditures of more than a billion dollars went to Alaska from 1941 to 1945, and the boom changed Alaska permanently.[1]

The most dramatic recognition of the importance of northern geography was in the ferrying of aircraft to the Soviet Union to help that nation's fight against Germany. Planes started from Great Falls, Montana, and followed the route of the Alaska Highway to Fairbanks. Russian pilots took over the aircraft in Fairbanks, or in Nome, and completed the passage to Siberia. In all, the route was 1,900 miles long—a mere hop, on a global scale. A total of 7,926 aircraft of various types were delivered to Russia by way of Alaska.[2]

The Japanese had no intention of using the Aleutians as a springboard for a continental invasion: their campaign there was a diversion calculated to draw the United States fleet out of Pearl Harbor for the Japanese fleet to attack. Unfortunately for the reputation of Japanese strategists, the American navy steamed away from Hawaii to smash the enemy in the battle of Midway—the turning point of the Pacific war.

The Japanese landed on Attu and Kiska without meeting any resistance. The soldiers rounded up the Aleut residents and eventually sent them to Japan. Construction of airfields commenced, but the climate, a shortage of equipment, and the harassment of American bombers slowed progress. The Japanese failed to regain the incentive of their initial air attack and had no real purpose in hanging on after their diversionary function had been fulfilled; yet their orders were to fight on.

Aleutian weather has often been called the worst in the world. Certainly it hampered the air and naval operations of both combatants. More American planes crashed because of fog and gales than were destroyed by enemy gunfire. Unable to sight enemy fleets to engage in battle, ship commanders faced constant frustration.

In January 1943, American troops landed on Amchitka, an island sixty miles east of Kiska. The Americans constructed an

1. Brian Garfield's *The Thousand-Mile War* (New York: Doubleday, 1969) is a lively account of the Aleutian campaign.

2. Deane R. Brandon, "War Planes to Russia," *Alaska Magazine,* May 1976, pp. 14–17.

airfield within weeks and started bombing Kiska whenever the weather permitted flying. Attu Island was not subjected to the same harassment, because the American command planned an amphibious invasion and hoped that the Japanese would assume that Kiska would be the target.

While preparations for the Attu landing were going on, the opposing navies fought a battle that brought some glory to the Americans. In an effort to intercept supply ships, an American fleet took on a superior Japanese force in March 1943 off the Komandorski Islands. The opposing ships battered each other for hours with long-range guns. The American attack forced Japanese supply ships to return to the Kurile Islands without landing their cargoes.

Attu's invasion occurred in May of 1943 when 11,000 U.S. troops landed on opposite ends of the small island. Initially, the invaders made little progress against the well-fortified defenders. Within a week, however, the Americans pinched in the enemy between two landing forces. The Japanese could either surrender or die—and they preferred to die. All hospital patients committed suicide or were killed by their comrades. All the soldiers able to move charged toward the Americans. The suicidal affair was over quickly. Only 28 prisoners were taken; 2,351 Japanese died in the attack. American casualties ran high enough—549 dead, 1,148 wounded, and 932 disabled by exposure, accidents, and other causes. The percentage of casualties in the battle on Attu was higher than that of any other engagement of the Pacific war, except for that over Iwo Jima.

Now it was Kiska's turn. From June through August of 1943, Americans flew 1,454 bombing sorties over the island. In July, a heavy naval-ship bombardment pounded at the defenders in preparation for invasion.

During the same month, an American fleet fought the "Battle of the Pips." The U.S. Navy flagship, the *New Mexico,* supposedly made radar contact with a Japanese fleet, and the Americans fired a thousand shells on the enemy ships. When visibility improved, observer planes found no debris or shattered ships within the target area, nor any sign that their victims rested on the bottom of the sea. In fact, the radar had been misread; the

Americans had battled a phantom during the time that the real Japanese fleet had passed unseen through the blockade of Kiska.

That event discouraged the American command, but the American invasion of Kiska resulted in even more humiliation. After all the bombing raids and naval bombardments, 35,000 American and Canadian soldiers waded ashore, exchanged shots with each other, tripped mines to produce 313 casualties, and searched for the enemy. They discovered two dogs, but the Japanese forces had been evacuated. That unnecessary invasion ended the Aleutian campaign.

The Kiska campaign served as a classic example of poor military planning on both sides. The Japanese feint toward Alaska failed to produce the desired effect. The American army sent poorly prepared troops to invade fog-bound islands of no particular value. If the Japanese had been ignored, they could have done little harm and might have been recalled. Aleutian weather provided the best defense against air attacks, and the Japanese had few planes. But Alaska was American soil, so the invaders had to be expelled.

In the 1930s, the world knew Alaska only as an isolated and sparsely populated frontier with a population of about sixty-five thousand. The territory held only seven cities with more than a thousand people, and only twenty-five hundred miles of public highways. The highway mileage was significant—in the states, the same mileage serviced an area of approximately thirty-six square miles. For years, the American and Canadian governments had been considering the construction of a highway to Alaska, but it took the Japanese attack on Pearl Harbor to get the project started.

Early in 1942, work began on a pioneer road from Dawson Creek, British Columbia, to Big Delta, Alaska. The existing northern Canadian highway system ended at Dawson Creek, and Alaska's Richardson Highway between Valdez and Fairbanks could be connected to the new road with a junction at Big Delta. The U.S. Army Corps of Engineers directed the work of nine thousand soldiers, mostly black, and of twelve thousand civilians who, despite the harsh climate and difficult terrain, put the road through in just nine months.

The pioneer road was slashed through by twenty-one-ton bulldozers that uprooted trees and brush with wide-cutting blades, leaving a fifty- to one-hundred-foot clearing. Other bulldozers followed and leveled the right of way. Culvert gangs cut trees and built square, green-log culverts fastened with steel drift pins. In areas needing fills, carryalls pulled by tractors hauled material from the hills that they simply cut through. Finished grading followed rough leveling. Alluvial riverbeds or hillsides supplied the necessary gravel.

The men had to fight many hazards. Frozen ground, once stripped of its vegetative cover, quickly turned into muck and had to be corduroyed with poles laid side by side across the track and covered with gravel. Equipment easily became mired in the muck. Countless mosquitoes made life extremely uncomfortable for the soldiers, who wore close-meshed nets for protection over their broad-brimmed, World War I-style campaign hats. As the summer wore on, truck convoys stirred up clouds of fine dust that made breathing difficult, covered everything, and penetrated everywhere. With the coming of winter, temperatures dropped, daylight waned, and soldiers experienced bone-chilling temperatures of fifty degrees below zero and lower. At those temperatures, equipment balked and broke down often. Yet speed was all-important because of the short northern season. The pioneer road had many steep curves, and only minimum attention was given to cuts and fills. Trestles of native spruce spanned the streams, and in many sections boggy ground made the road extremely unstable, while stream overflows built up thick layers of ice on the road. Despite its shortcomings, however, the 1,420-mile-long pioneer road, built under extraordinarily difficult conditions and in record time, represented a major engineering feat.

America's improved military position in the Aleutians and the Pacific in early 1943 relieved the pressure for rapid completion of the highway, but it was still considered essential that a permanent road be completed. Some 11,107 pieces of equipment, trucks, tractors, crushers, graders, and bulldozers, worked along the 1,420 miles of the route to complete the job by December 1943 at a cost of nearly $20 million.

The road had been built for military purposes but was opened to civilian use in 1948. The existence of a road to the states had a significant psychological effect on Alaskans of the interior. The road link greatly reduced the sense of isolation that Alaskans felt in the winter after river navigation closed. Moreover, the highway opened up thousands of square miles to potential development. It also gave Alaskans an alternative to ocean-freight transportation. During a maritime strike in 1946, goods hauled over the highway prevented the complete economic paralysis of the territory. Two major sea-transport strikes occurred in 1952, lasting a total of eighty-six days. Airlines absorbed some of the extra load, while much necessary freight came over the highway.

Although military activities decreased rapidly in Alaska after 1943, the war had a profound and lasting impact on the territory. It irrevocably altered the pace and tenor of Alaskan life. Residual benefits to the civilian economy and the development of Alaska were tremendous. Between 1941 and 1945, the federal government spent well over one billion dollars in Alaska. The modernization of the Alaska Railroad, expansion of airfields, and construction of roads benefited the civilian population. Many of the docks, wharves, and breakwaters built along the coast for the use of the navy, the Coast Guard, and the Army Transport Service were turned over to the territory after the war. Thousands of soldiers and construction workers had come north. Many decided to make Alaska their home at the end of the hostilities, a fact reflected in population statistics: between 1940 and 1950, the territory's civilian population increased from roughly 74,000 to 112,000.

World War II brought to Alaska the biggest boom the territory had ever experienced, bigger than any of the gold rushes of the past. Yet, at the end of the war, with curtailment of defense spending, Alaskans once again were confronted with the problems of a seasonal economy.

At that juncture, tensions between the United States and the Soviet Union rescued Alaska from economic depression and obscurity. Alaska's geographical position astride the northern Great Circle gave the territory a strategic importance. The mili-

ALASKA

A photographer's essay by Yvonne Mozée

Photographs in sequence

December afternoon at Barrow.
Ready to start Iditarod Trail Race to Nome, Anchorage.
Near downtown Fairbanks.
Aleut bicyclist at Russian Orthodox church, Unalaska.
Erecting Alaska Centennial totem, Juneau.
Gambell Eskimo inspects stretched sealskin, meat drying in the
  background.
Parking at car heaters, Anchorage.
Front Street after summer rain, Nome.
Fourth Avenue, Anchorage.
Beach airstrip at Wales on the Bering Strait.
Goldstream dredge near Fairbanks, closed in 1963.
Welders' crew helpers, trans-Alaska pipeline construction near
  Galbraith Lake.
Troller at Elfin Cove, Mount Fairweather and Brady Glacier in background.
Processing king salmon aboard ship, Dutch Harbor.
Mount McKinley.

tary assigned thousands of troops to Alaska and continued to spend millions of defense dollars.

In 1949, military planners worried about Russian activities in Siberia and theorized that four-engined aircraft, stationed on the Chukotsk Peninsula, could attack the atomic bomb plant at Hanford, in the state of Washington, and return to their bases. American defenses in Alaska were weak. No infantry were based there, and Fairbanks and Anchorage maintained less than a hundred old jet fighters without sufficient range even to reach Nome and return to bases. A limited radar network existed, but much needed to be done to bring about effective improvement in Alaskan defenses.

The cold war forced American strategic revision, and in the late 1940s, military planners decided on the so-called heartland concept of Alaska defense. The idea included virtual abandonment of the Aleutian Islands and proposals for huge military bases near Fairbanks and Anchorage. The new concept coincided with a general realignment in over-all military strategy from the Pacific to the Atlantic.

Before the shift in emphasis could be accomplished, however, massive problems had to be overcome in Alaska. A region of magnificent distances, lethal cold, forbidding terrain, and a still totally inadequate system of communication and transportation, the territory challenged American technical imagination and ingenuity. Despite the intensive construction activity during World War II, Alaska still was a primitive frontier. The region lacked housing and had no modern economic and social infrastructure to support the defense effort. Additionally, the territory's difficult terrain and weather were permanent features always to be reckoned with.

Supplies still came mostly by sea from Seattle to the ports of Seward, Whittier, or Anchorage, each one insufficient in one way or another. Seward probably had the best port, although wood worms continually damaged the docks. Whittier, built during the war and located at the head of a fjord in a small glacial ravine, was plagued by high winds, almost continuous rain and snowfall, and by inadequate docking and unloading facilities. With a glacier behind it, the sea in front of it, and thirty to fifty feet of snow on top of it in the winter, it was isolated, had no recreational facilities, and appeared to be the end of nowhere in Alaska for army personnel unfortunate enough to serve there. Large ice floes and thirty-six-foot tides menaced shipping to Anchorage.

The Alaska Railroad, which carried freight from the ports, was antiquated by now. Completed in 1923, after eight years of construction, the railroad's average daily capacity of some fifteen hundred tons did not even meet prewar requirements. The railroad lacked equipment and operated over a poor roadbed. In the so-called loop area between Seward and Portage, the trains had to traverse a high ravine in an approximately 360-degree circle where high, wooden trestles, erected many years earlier and quite shaky by 1949, supported the tracks. Additionally, heavy snows and occasional avalanches between Seward and Anchorage interrupted train service often.

In order to realize the "heartland" concept of defense in Alaska, the military needed vast expenditures to provide basic facilities. The Defense Department asked Congress for funding, and although it delayed or cut various construction requests, military expenditures approached $100 million in 1949, which started the territory's postwar economic boom. In 1950, military spending increased to $250 million.

In 1940, the territory boasted 75,000 residents, of whom some 1,000 were military personnel. By 1950, Alaska's population had jumped to 138,000, including 26,000 servicemen. Anchorage, a sleepy railroad town of 3,495 in 1940, contained an estimated 11,060 residents in 1950, excluding several outlying suburbs that would have brought the population to some 20,000 souls. These figures also disregarded transients and military personnel stationed at the bases. Fairbanks's population jumped from approximately 5,600 in 1940 to 11,700 in 1950, and that of Seward from 949 to 2,063 during the same decade.

The massive infusion of military dollars stimulated tertiary growth. Builders raised modern hotels and office buildings, and new radio stations gained permission to operate. Air transportation vastly expanded with new commercial airports and connections to most points in Alaska and to many international destinations. Modern subdivisions alternated with unattractive slum areas with shacks and wanigans, largely the result of slipshod regulations and hurry-up building. In Fairbanks, bank deposits doubled from 1949 to 1952, while, in Anchorage, car registration increased by 1,390 percent in a decade, and school attendance rose by nearly 1,000 percent within the same period. The population of the greater Anchorage area increased some 52.5 percent between April 1, 1950, and December 31, 1951. Much remained to be done, in spite of the private building boom sparked by defense spending. Both major towns suffered from a shortage of school buildings, and Fairbanks direly needed a sewage disposal system. But, for the first time, Alaska offered bright opportunities for young professionals in addition to the customary seasonal employment for floating labor.

By 1954, the territory had passed the peak of military construction. Military housing needs had largely been met, and Alaska's defenses had nearly been completed with a network of radar stations and military bases. The gains had been great. Within a five-year period, from 1949 to 1954, the territory had become habitable on a year-round basis for a vastly increased population. Approximately $250 million per year had been spent from 1949 to 1954 for military and civilian construction combined.

Probably no other part of America was affected more by World War II than Alaska. During that time, Alaskans were not supported primarily by a resource extraction industry, but by government and defense-related activities. But despite the vast sums of federal money brought in by war activities, the shift in economic emphasis consisted more of form than substance. Instead of exploiting gold, the government had turned to another natural resource: geographic location. Strategic demands dictated that Alaska be the outer bastion of continental defenses against a trans-Arctic attack. If, later, the military decided that Alaska need not be defended, the boom would be followed by a bust in the familiar historical pattern. Despite its population growth, Alaska still lacked a stable economic base.

In 1957, Richfield Oil Company discovered oil at Swanson River on the Kenai Peninsula, and by 1959 three wells were operating on the site. Exploration and development activities extended to offshore Cook Inlet, where soon additional oil and gas fields were brought into production. At the end of the 1960s, five fields in the Kenai-Cook Inlet area produced oil, and nine fields yielded natural gas. By then, wildcatters were drilling holes at various locations throughout Alaska.[3]

These were not the first discoveries of petroleum in Alaska, however. In the early part of the twentieth century, wildcatters drilled near Cold Bay on the Alaska Peninsula and in the Katalla district on the coast of the Gulf of Alaska, east of Cordova. A refinery built in 1911 utilized a small Katalla oil discovery, and during the next twenty years, about 150,000 barrels were produced. The operation ended when the refinery burned in 1931.[4]

Early in the nineteenth century, travelers had reported oil seepages on Alaska's North Slope. Standard Oil Company of California had explored for North Slope Oil near Cape Simpson in 1921, guided by prospector Sandy Smith, who had stumbled into oil seepage there three years earlier. Private development stopped, however, when President Warren G. Harding designated 37,000 square miles on the North Slope as Naval Petroleum Reserve No. 4. The U.S. Geological Survey investigated the area from 1923 to 1926, and the navy searched for oil from 1944 to 1953. The search revealed that a major petroleum province existed, but no major discoveries occurred.

In 1968, Atlantic Richfield made its momentous strike at Prudhoe Bay on the Arctic coast, and suddenly, Alaska boomed. The North Slope discovery quickened the pace of oil exploration all over the state, and good prospects have been reported in the Yukon Valley and elsewhere. In addition, estimates of the potential yield of the outer continental shelf vary, but it appears to be enough to maintain production for many years.

3. Gordon Harrison, editor, *Alaska Public Policy* (Fairbanks: Institute of Social, Economic and Government Research, 1971), pp. 31–32, 182–183; Ernest W. Mueller, "Alaskan Oil—the Energy Crisis and the Environment," *Arctic Bulletin* 1, no. 5: 185–186.

4. Harrison, *Alaska Public Policy,* pp. 31–32, 182–183.

11

Long Haul to Statehood

$\mathcal{A}$LASKA joined the Union as the forty-ninth state in 1959, after several years of intense political activity by partisans of statehood. The territory's slow, uncertain progress to political maturity paralleled its halting course to achieve a solid economy. In many respects, these major goals were intertwined, particularly as a weak economy and small population served as rationalizations for delaying self-rule.

In 1867, Secretary of State William H. Seward arranged for the U.S. Army to govern the newly acquired possession. He reasoned that congressional action would soon follow, and what he designated a customs district would be granted territorial status. Seward reassured discontented Alaskans of Sitka in 1869 that "the political society to be constituted here, first as a territory, and ultimately as a state or many states, will prove a worthy constituency of the Republic." [1] But Seward's vision of a timely transition from customs district to territory and, finally, to statehood, proved faulty. Despite Alaska's prodigious size and rich resources and counter to the hopes of its residents, the political transformation faltered along at a discouraging pace. Alaska waited ninety years for its place in the Union. After Congress acted in 1870 to lease the Pribilof Islands, no other

1. William H. Seward, *Speech at Sitka, August 12, 1869* (Washington, D.C.: Philip and Soloman, 1869), p. 16.

117

substantial Alaskan legislation surfaced until 1884. Until enactment of the Organic Act of 1884 and subsequent legislation inspired by the Klondike gold rush, Alaskans had no local laws enabling them legally to stake mining claims, acquire land title, enforce contracts, bequeath property, or marry.

Why such apparent neglect? Congressional apathy rested in the irrelevancy of Alaska in a Gilded-Age America preoccupied with restoration, industrialization, urbanization, "and a contiguous West rich in mines, farming, and cattle, everywhere being tied together by a burgeoning railroad network." [2]

But these explanations, reasonable as they seemed, scarcely satisfied the pleas of Alaskans in the late 1870s and early 1880s when the governmental presence existed only in a few customs officials and navy personnel. White citizens of Sitka considered that their government let them down in withdrawing the military in 1877. Sitkans feared massacre by restive Indians and ultimately appealed to the British navy for help.

The discovery of gold near the present site of Juneau in 1880 finally prompted Congress to pass an Organic Act for Alaska in 1884. That fundamental law made Alaska a civil and judicial district. A presidentially appointed governor possessed few specific powers, while a judge, district attorney, marshal, four deputy marshals, a clerk, and four commissioners enforced United States laws and, wherever applicable, the general laws of the state of Oregon. The United States circuit court for the district of Oregon was to hear appeals from decisions of Alaska's district court. Congress extended United States mining laws to its northern territory as a land district but withheld the general land laws for the time being. Finally, the Organic Act provided that Alaskan natives were not to be disturbed in the possession of any lands actually in their use or occupation or then claimed by them. Final disposition of such claims rested on future congressional action. Clearly, the Organic Act of 1884 was sketchy and makeshift. It had omitted to provide either a legislature or congressional representation. The law levied no taxes and made no provision for establishing towns or counties.

2. Hinckley, *Americanization of Alaska,* pp. 24–25.

Under the Oregon Code, applicable to Alaska as well, only county superintendents could establish school districts; hence, no school districts could be formed in Alaska. No jury trials could be held, because the same code required the selection of jurors from among taxpayers.

Although there were other inequities, the first Organic Act did provide Alaska with the rudiments of a governmental structure. But Alaskans, like pioneers on other American frontiers, clamored for additional legislation. Although the northern pioneers were few in number, they could point to a growing gold-mining industry and a salmon industry that had packed some 966,707 forty-eight-pound cases of salmon in the years from 1878 to 1896.

Population statistics reflected economic activities. In 1890, the census had listed a population of 32,052; in 1900, it had grown to 63,592. The 1896 gold discovery near the Klondike, a tributary of the Yukon River in Canada's Yukon Territory, had much to do with the population increase. Soon afterwards—in 1898—restless argonauts discovered gold on the Seward Peninsula, which resulted in the famous Nome rush of 1899–1900. Gold found in the Tanana valley in 1902 resulted in the establishment of the towns of Chena and Fairbanks.

The subsequent influx of people moved Congress to action. Between 1897 and 1901, Congress supplemented the Organic Act of 1884 with a transportation and homestead act (1898), a criminal code and code of criminal procedure (1899), and a civil code and code of civil procedure (1900). These pieces of legislation provided Alaska with a more adequate civil government. Congress divided Alaska into three judicial divisions. Communities of at least three hundred residents could now incorporate, and there were provisions for the establishment of municipal and district schools. Alaska's capital was to be moved from Sitka to Juneau whenever suitable grounds and buildings had been obtained. That took place in 1900, although it was 1906 before the change could be called completed. In short, Alaskans now possessed criminal and civil laws, means for their enforcement, limited local self-government, and a rudimentary system of taxation.

Still, Alaskan residents called for broader powers at home and for a delegate to represent them in Congress. The Northwest Ordinance, approved by the Congress of the Confederation in 1787, had provided for government of the territory north of the Ohio River and for territorial representation by a voteless delegate. The office had evolved slowly over the years, and in 1808 the delegateship first became popularly elective in the Territory of Mississippi.[3] Seated in the House of Representatives, the delegate enjoyed all the rights and privileges of a congressman—except the right to vote. The delegate also represented his territory before the executive branch of the federal government and acquainted his constituents with national politics. Since he was voteless, much of the delegate's effectiveness depended upon his ability to persuade and to make friends.

Over the years, Congress usually had authorized a territorial legislature before providing for the election of a delegate. By 1903, however, Alaskans had received a pledge from President Theodore Roosevelt for congressional representation. Alaskans desired representation and differed only on the method of selecting a delegate. A majority preferred election, while a minority, fearing inordinate election expenses in such a vast area, favored presidential appointment with senatorial consent.

In 1904, the House passed a delegate bill that Senator Orville Platt of Connecticut opposed when it reached the upper chamber. Platt wanted to insure that granting delegate representation would not imply later admission to statehood. Interior Alaska's popular Judge James Wickersham, who had favorably testified for the measure earlier, before Congress, now asked if it would be necessary for Alaska to form an independent republic with its own constitution and divide into four states, namely Sitka, Alaska, Sumner, and Tanana. It would be preferable, he argued, to admit the four states, once they had attained the necessary population, into the Union of the United States. Nothing happened, however.

After achieving congressional representation in 1906, some

3. U.S., *Statutes at Large*, 1 Stat. 52; Max Farrand, *The Legislation of Congress for the Government of the Organized Territories of the United States, 1789–1895* (Newark: William R. Baker, 1896), p. 18.

Alaskans demanded a territorial legislature. James Wickersham led the battle, after being elected delegate in 1908. The appointed governor, Wilford B. Hoggatt (1906–1910), opposed it, and so did powerful commercial interests. Cannery owners and the Morgan-Guggenheim syndicate that dominated shipping and mining feared that a territorial legislature would levy taxes on their operations.

Hoggatt assured President Theodore Roosevelt that "It is the consensus of opinion [*sic*] of the conservative businessmen of Alaska, those men who are doing the most for the development of the country, that the time is inopportune for this form of government." The existing system of federal control was "the best possible" for meeting all needs: "It is inexpensive, certain, and capable of expansion as the needs of the country justify." Alaska's population at the time was considered too small to support home rule, and "a large portion of the agitation for territorial government comes from the saloon element . . . which is desirous of decreasing the burdens now imposed upon that business and at the same time obtaining a greater liberty than they now have in the conduct of their business." [4] Attributing support for home rule to the "saloon element" did not make the governor popular in Alaska.

Hoggatt had traveled extensively in Alaska and felt that he appreciated the people's needs. His very liberal estimate of the population reinforced his convictions on home rule. Southeastern Alaska had nine thousand residents; the Seward Peninsula and the Arctic had twelve thousand; and the interior and Southcentral together had another twelve thousand.

Alaskans who longed for home rule received a painful shock in 1909, when President William H. Taft made known his plans for the region. For some obscure reason, Taft equated Alaska with the Philippine Islands, where he had served as commissioner, and thought both places should be administered by the Department of War. Alaska Road Commissioner Major Wilds P. Richardson considered Taft's scheme a splendid idea and

4. Jeannette Paddock Nichols, *Alaska: A History of Its Administration, Exploitation, and Industrial Development during Its First Half Century under the Rule of the United States* (Cleveland: Arthur H. Clark Co., 1924), pp. 279–280.

helped prepare legislation that Senator Albert J. Beveridge (R., Indiana) introduced in the Senate. Alaska's delegate to Congress, James Wickersham, was furious when he heard that a senate committee was reviewing the military bill and had quite deliberately resolved not to call on him for consultation. Wickersham was not noted for reticence. He forced his way past the guard at the committee-room door and demanded a copy of the bill from Beveridge. After reading it hurriedly, he lashed out at its contents and questioned the patriotism and sanity of its authors.

Wickersham was somewhat paranoid about the Morgan-Guggenheim Syndicate, which dominated mining and shipping in the North; he believed that it was behind the military commission plan. The Syndicate could deal with the military in a pleasant way and would never need to fear the specter of a territorial legislature burdening its mining and shipping operations with taxation or other controls. Albert Fink, a lobbyist hired by the Syndicate, pretended to be nothing more than an interested, intelligent resident of Nome when he appeared in Washington to testify. (An attorney, Fink later gained fame as Al Capone's defense lawyer). Fink solemnly assured Congress that most Alaskans wintered Outside and were actually only seasonal workers in the North. Transients, he insisted, should not have the responsibility of making laws for Alaska—the military could do much better. Fink also appealed to the committee's distaste for radical unionism. Most miners, argued Fink, belonged to the notorious Western Federation of Miners, and they did not elect the proper kind of men to union leadership.

The Beveridge bill died in the committee after Wickersham exposed one of its provisions that would have given the Syndicate the opportunity to lease five thousand acres of coal land adjacent to the Cunningham claims in Alaska. (Earlier comment on the coal-claims controversy appears in chapter 9.) That arrangement was too blatant an exertion of monopolistic intent and political jobbery to withstand scrutiny, and Beveridge had to give up on Taft's military scheme. Taft did not give up his plan, but he was kept on the defensive for the rest of his term by Progressives who hoped to hound him out of office. Wickersham pursued his attempt to get an elective territorial legislature bill for Alaska through the Congress and was successful in the 1912 session.

The 1912 Second Organic Act designated Alaska as an incorporated territory and cleared the way for eventual admission to the Union. It comprised a significant milestone in progress toward full self-government. Now Alaskans could elect local representatives and hope for a more responsive government. Legislative authority was limited. The federally appointed governor held veto powers and Congress could disapprove the action of a territorial legislature. But the 1912 federal legislation definitely ended the confusion regarding Alaska's status and stated that "the Constitution . . . shall have the same force and effect within the Territory of Alaska as elsewhere in the United States." [5]

Another confusion cleared by the Second Organic Act proceeded from the earlier designation of Alaska as a district rather than a territory. By declaring Alaska a territory in 1912, Congress removed an impediment to self-rule. In the so-called Insular Cases of 1901, the Supreme Court had distinguished between unincorporated and incorporated territories. Puerto Rico, unlike Alaska, was adjudged unincorporated, and thus unlikely to become a state. The nebulous distinction between incorporated and unincorporated prompted Secretary of War Elihu Root's remark that "as near as I can make out the constitution follows the flag—but doesn't quite catch up with it." [6]

In 1916, Alaskan Delegate James Wickersham introduced the territory's first statehood bill. Alaska's population stood at fifty-eight thousand, and most residents remained indifferent to statehood. A more heated issue stimulated controversy in the 1920s, as Alaskans of the southeastern Panhandle, where the majority of the population lived, called for secession from the rest of Alaska. These secession advocates had been impressed by President Warren G. Harding's indication that southeastern Alaska might be set apart and thus achieve statehood before the less

5. Claus-M. Naske, *An Interpretative History of Alaskan Statehood* (Anchorage: Alaska Northwest Publishing Co., 1973), p. 7.

6. Naske, *Interpretative History*, p. 8.

populous parts of the territory. Yet early statehood motivated
them less than a desire to avoid sharing revenues with the poor,
less populous sections of the territory. Congress ignored the
secessionists, and the territory remained intact.

With the abrupt increase in population occasioned by World
War II, a greater awareness of the importance of statehood developed. From 1943 to 1953, the movement was spearheaded
by the territory's governor, the congressional delegate, and a
small but diversified group of business and professional persons.
In 1946, a referendum indicated that 60 percent of Alaskans
favored statehood. The territorial legislature acted in 1949 to establish an official Alaskan Statehood Committee. As was the
custom in Alaskan matters Congress held hearings in 1947.
Most witnesses praised and supported the aspirations of statehood supporters.

As historian Claus-M. Naske has pointed out in his study of
Alaskan statehood, it was essential that Alaska put its own
house in order by providing an adequate tax system. On attain-
ing statehood, Alaska would have to assume the burden of services previously supported by the national government. Mining
and canning lobbyists and wealthy Alaskans, like Fairbanks entrepreneur Austin Lathrop and the Lomens of Nome, who dominated Seward Peninsula commerce, felt threatened by the possi-
bility of taxation and opposed such measures vigorously.
Lathrop opposed statehood as well, insisting as late as 1949 that
if it were achieved he would immediately sell out all his interests for fifty cents on the dollar.

In the late 1930s, a tax study indicated that it would be possible to raise an annual revenue of $10 million through a rational
tax system. The appraised value of the physical properties of the
mining and canning industries alone was estimated at more than
a half-billion dollars in the 1940s. A tax of 1 percent on these
assets would have given the territory $5 million a year. More
revenue could have been brought in by taxing the profits of con-
tractors and the incomes of their employees. But Alaska strug-
gled on without those revenues, and the biennial expenditures of
the territory were slim indeed. From 1933 to 1935, Alaska spent
a little over $2 million; ten years later, the expenditures rose to

$5.5 million, but that amount was far too little to support services.

Even after territorial Governor Ernest Gruening guided a tax-reform bill through the legislature in 1949, the special interests still waxed fat. In 1947, journalist Richard L. Neuberger had described Alaska as the looted land, a feudal barony where absentee entrepreneurs carried away millions in natural resources and left virtually nothing in return. Alaskans owned only 38 of the 434 fish traps licensed by the United States Department of the Interior. The value of the fish pack in 1946 was $56,571,000, on which the territorial tax was a modest $630,000. Taxes on gear and traps added to territorial revenues, but the total tax bite was light. That year, the fishing industry brought 12,484 workers to Alaska and paid them $7,206,000 in wages, none of which was taxed because the employees were paid at their point of hire, after the canning season. Alaskans hired by the packing industry that year numbered only 10,956, and their combined earnings were $3,729,000.[7]

The Alaska Steamship Company and the Northland Transportation Company dominated shipping, and both granted preferential freight rates to the canneries. Canneries paid $14.23 a ton for freight, while other Alaskan customers paid twice that amount. There was no option, because both shipping companies were owned by the Skinner family and held a monopoly over northern business.

Lobbyists were finally quelled after the 1948 territorial election. The voters, educated by Gruening and others, sent legislators to Juneau resolved to rectify the scandalous tax situation. The legislature passed a territorial income tax bill and modified the existing business license fee system to provide for taxation of enterprises that had always escaped taxes previously. In effect, the legislature, which met in Juneau early in 1949, set the territorial house in order and prepared Alaska for statehood.

In 1950, a statehood bill passed in the U.S. House for the first time and hearings were scheduled for the Senate Interior and Insular Affairs Committee. The Seattle-based salmon in-

7. Naske, *Interpretative History,* p. 86.

dustry fought fiercely against statehood for Alaska, because cannery operators feared state control of the fisheries and the abolition of fish traps. Winton C. Arnold, director of the trade association of the industry, appeared for the cannery operators, armed with charts and graphs indicating the woes that Alaska would encounter if admitted to the Union. Alaska could not support the services the state would have to undertake, charged Arnold. He also observed that international treaties could be impaired, that the aboriginal land claims would lead to complete confusion, and that federal lands could not be transferred to the state because surveys had not been made. Arnold never admitted that he opposed statehood; he objected only to the particular bill under consideration. An intelligent and effective lobbyist, he received credit from the proponents of statehood for the defeat of the 1950 bill in the Senate.

In 1952, the U.S. Senate once again considered statehood. Senator Hugh Butler (R., Nebraska) reiterated Arnold's criticism of the bill at length. He piously confessed to a deep emotional feeling for Alaska and hoped his colleagues would not charge a mere 108,000 Alaskans with the costs of statehood. Butler derided statehood proponents who had appeared at hearings: these witnesses, he said, came "at the taxpayer's expense to present us with their reasons for desiring statehood." [8]

Senator Warren Magnuson (D., Washington) favored statehood and made it clear where much of the opposition came from. When asked who had voted against statehood in a territorial referendum held in 1946, he replied: "Most of the votes in opposition . . . came from my own home town of Seattle, and were stirred up by a very small group of people." [9] Seattlelites who earned their incomes in Alaska wished to preserve the status quo and had manipulated the 1946 election, Magnuson explained.

In his autobiography, *Many Battles,* Alaskan Territorial Governor Ernest Gruening told of a lecture that he gave U.S. Defense Department officials and Congressmen in Seattle. At issue was the government's plan, announced in August 1949, to have

8. Naske, *Interpretative History,* p. 105.
9. Naske, *Interpretative History,* p. 106.

the Boeing Airplane Company close its Seattle plant and move its operation to Wichita, Kansas, where it would be less vulnerable to a Soviet air attack. Gruening argued that such a move made little sense, because the Soviets were capable of extending the range of their bombers. The governor suggested that radar stations be constructed along the northern and western coasts and that plenty of interceptor aircraft be stationed in Alaska. "Incredible as it may seem," Gruening wrote later, "my suggestion for a radar screen was apparently a new idea to military planners." [10] Whether he was correct in that surmise or not, action followed swiftly. The U.S. Air Force rescinded its plans of moving Boeing and three months later announced that $50 million had been allotted to build the Distant Early Warning System along the Arctic and Bering seacoasts. The line of stations was eventually extended all the way across the Canadian Arctic coast, as well.

The construction boom that followed during the next several years of building the DEW line and the Ballistic Missile Early Warning System base at Clear, Alaska (a station near Fairbanks linked with similar stations in England and Greenland built when strategic emphasis shifted from aircraft to missile defense), saved Alaska from a postwar economic collapse. It also encouraged advocates of statehood to press their case.

They could argue more effectively that Alaska was ready for statehood because its economy was bolstered by construction and military payrolls, and its population had increased. Gruening, who had cautioned against statehood until he became a total convert in 1945, expected the Seattle Chamber of Commerce to endorse the cause. He reasoned that he had saved Boeing, Seattle's largest employer, by his DEW-line proposal, and the city's businessmen should reciprocate. But the Seattle Chamber of Commerce refused their support. Seattle business interests had dominated the Alaskan trade since the Klondike gold rush of 1897–1898, and they feared the restrictions and taxes a state might impose upon them. Gruening was rueful: "The so-called Alaska Committee of the Seattle Chamber of Commerce is

10. Ernest Gruening, *Many Battles: The Autobiography of Ernest Gruening* (New York: Liveright, 1973), p. 362.

dominated by men who view Alaska as King George the Third and his ministers viewed the Thirteen Colonies, an area to be ruled and exploited by distant men through their representation in the colony, but never to be treated on a basis of equality.'' [11] Seattle's attitude was clear. The Puget Sound city wished to maintain the status quo.

A coalition of southern and conservative senators, who assumed Alaska's representatives would be Democrats, opposed statehood and effectively delayed the bill in 1952. The measure was returned to the Senate Committee on Interior and Insular Affairs by a vote of forty-five to forty-four. The House decided against considering the bill because of the Senate's action.

In 1953, Senator Hugh Butler and other senators held hearings in Alaska on the statehood issue. These hearings resulted in a ground swell of sentiment for statehood among Alaskans. The senators heard 140 witnesses, of whom fewer than 20 opposed statehood. Those in opposition were, for the most part, older and well-established Alaskans who were concerned about new taxes. Those supporting the bill included most of the younger group of Alaskans who migrated to the territory after World War II. These new Alaskans expressed themselves militantly against statehood opponents and a federal government that denied them the full rights of citizenship.

Butler apparently did not receive the message delivered by Alaskans at the hearings. He returned to Nebraska to announce that most of ''the clamor for statehood came from politicians who wanted to run for office.'' [12] Democratic senators who participated in the hearings disagreed vigorously with Butler and pointed out that virtually all the Alaskans encountered demanded statehood at once.

No progress was made toward statehood in Congress in 1954 or 1955. President Dwight Eisenhower favored statehood for Hawaii but opposed it for Alaska. Two considerations influenced the president: he felt that, in a defense emergency, the military could function better if Alaska remained a territory; and he also wanted to protect the narrow Republican majority in the

11. Gruening, *Many Battles*, p. 363.
12. Naske, *Interpretative History*, p. 119.

Senate. It was then the political assumption that Alaska's representation would be Democratic and Hawaii's Republican.

Alaskans had the inspiration of holding a constitutional convention in 1955. The territorial legislature appropriated $300,000 to hire consultants to advise the convention. Elected convention members met in Fairbanks in November 1955 to draw up a constitution. After seventy-five working days, a brief document of 14,400 words, described by the National Municipal League as "one of the best, if not the best, state constitutions ever written," was drafted and approved.[13] The constitution provided for a governor, a bicameral legislature, a unified judicial system, and other elements of a political structure for the future state. The document was offered to the voters of Alaska for their ratification.

Convention delegates also asked voters to approve of the Tennessee Plan for gaining admission to the Union. Tennessee had been granted statehood after an elected delegation had been sent to Washington in 1796 to plead for admission. Alaskan voters approved the newly drafted constitution overwhelmingly and endorsed the Tennessee Plan, as well. In the October 1956 election, Alaskans elected three Democrats for the Tennessee Plan positions: Ernest Gruening, William Egan, and Ralph Rivers.

Congress refused to seat Alaska's delegation but these "delegates" and other Alaskans lobbied intensively in Washington from 1956 to 1958. National sentiment strongly favored statehood. A Gallup poll of late 1955 had shown that 82 percent of Americans supported the admission of Alaska. Senate sentiment began to swing in favor of admission, too. Alaska's cause received a powerful boost when House Speaker Sam Rayburn dropped his opposition to the bill that would grant statehood. In June 1957, the House Interior and Insular Affairs Committee recommended admission, but consideration by the House was deferred until 1958. The House voted favorably, and the bill was sent to the Senate.

Southern senators tried to defeat the bill, although they realized that that would be impossible. By a vote of sixty-four to

13. Naske, *Interpretative History,* p. 143.

twenty the Senate voted in favor on June 30, 1958. Alaskans cheered over their triumph: after nearly a century of wardship, they finally had gained full political participation the Union. President Eisenhower formally admitted the forty-ninth state on January 3, 1959.

Alaska's dependence on the federal government did not end with statehood. The new state's economic weakness was demonstrated dramatically by a natural catastrophe.

On March 27, 1964, the greatest earthquake ever to rock a portion of North America shook the towns of Anchorage, Valdez, and Kodiak to pieces. The Richter scale, which measures the energy of an earthquake at its source, showed a reading of between 8.3 and 8.6, and the duration of the shock was remarkable—a good three minutes. Probably twice as much energy was released as in the earthquake that devastated San Francisco in 1906. According to the report published by the National Academy of Sciences,

> The shock was felt . . . over 500,000 miles. A tsunami (a train of long waves impulsively generated, in this case by movement of the sea floor) or "tidal wave" swept from the Gulf of Alaska across the length of the Pacific and lapped against Antarctica. Water levels in wells as far away as South Africa jumped abruptly, and shock-induced waves were generated in the Gulf of Mexico. An atmospheric pressure wave caused by the earthquake was recorded at La Jolla, California, more than 2,000 miles away. Seismic surface waves, with periods of many seconds, gently displaced the ground surface of most of the North American continent by as much as 2 inches.[14]

The shock did considerable damage to the land and to wildlife. Salmon spawning-beds were covered with silt, salmon fry were killed, forests were leveled, salt water was swept into many fresh-water lakes, birds' nesting grounds and the habitats of fish and shellfish were disturbed with a resulting loss of life that is incalculable. Men actually suffered less than did nature and wildlife. Nonetheless, 115 people were killed in Alaska, and

---

14. National Academy of Sciences, *Great Alaska Earthquake of 1964: Human Ecology,* (Washington, D.C.: National Academy of Sciences, 1970), p. 1.

another 16 perished in Oregon and California. If the population had been greater or if other factors had been different—the timing of the quake, the low tide, good weather, and the absence of fires—the story would have been one of mass tragedy. Luckily, the quake struck at 5:36 P.M., a time when the schools and most offices were closed, the fishing fleet was not at sea, and the canneries were not operating. The property losses amounted to some $300 million. Hundreds of homes and other structures were shattered, and the town of Valdez was inundated by the sweeping tsunami.

Senator E. L. Bartlett of Alaska drafted a relief bill and guided it through the Senate with fellow Senator Ernest Gruening's help. When the latter rose in the U.S. Senate to tell his colleagues that the catastrophe "surpasses in magnitude that suffered by any state of the Union in our Nation's entire history," the other senators rallied to his support. Senator Wayne Morse (D., Oregon) urged that federal funds be made available at once to rehabilitate Alaska. Senator Olin Johnston commented: "If this tragedy had struck some other nation . . . aid by the United States would have been rushed there immediately." [15] Let's take immediate steps to get help to Alaska, urged Johnston. Other senators quickly expressed sympathy and assured the senators from Alaska that they would give support.

In a later session, Gruening commended President Lyndon Johnson for his quick relief action. As soon as the president heard about the earthquake, he mobilized the Office of Emergency Planning and sent its director to Alaska. After the director reported back, Johnson called in the Alaska delegation for a meeting with the budget director and others. A good deal of money was needed, and Johnson meant to provide it. Meanwhile, Alaska's Governor William A. Egan flew to Washington, as soon as conditions settled down a bit in the disaster area, with a request for $500 million in aid. Housing loans or grants were the first priority, followed by requests for new port facilities for Valdez, Seward, and Kodiak.

15. U.S., Congress, Senate, *Congressional Record,* 88th Cong., 2d sess., 30 March 1964, 110, pt. 5:6494.

But for the generous flow of federal funds to individuals who lost homes and boats, to businessmen, and to those responsible for repairing public facilities like the Alaska Railroad and various airports, the disaster would have been a retarding blow to the young state. Money was tight at the time, and the state legislature had already been severely hard put, trying to find means for financing education, social services, and maintenance. The quake came a short time before the opening of the tourist season and, naturally, affected that source of income adversely. A recovery of the fisheries was essential, and the burning question was whether the federal government would react fast and generously enough to replace damaged trawlers, gill-netters, and other fishing boats. State officials forecasted a 20 percent loss in tax income for the coming fiscal year—a drop that would have hurt very much.

While all the negotiation for relief funds was going on, the world's press descended upon Anchorage. Of course, the newsmen wrote the kind of leads their readers anticipated. "This savage country," wrote a reporter for the *Washington Daily News,* "makes stoic people. They accept the majestic and cruel indifference of nature matter-of-factly." The article offered many examples of stoicism and of the Alaskan tendency to "hold nature in awed respect." [16]

As early as April 1, the *Washington Post* was able to report on the extent of aid to the stricken state. Tax relief was to be provided. A center for emergency housing loans was being set up in Anchorage. The Small Business Administration had its men on the way to make disaster loans. "The Military Air Transport Service, the Navy, the Air Force, and commerical lines are continuing a giant airlift of medicines, food, clothing, and every conceivable kind of equipment needed to make comfortable the thousands who have been living primitively since homes were destroyed." [17] And the fishing industry had been assured low-interest loans and perhaps direct subsidies for reconstruction. In all, seventeen grant agencies were directed by the federal relief co-ordinator to indicate what they could do to assist. In addition to all the government relief, charitable organi-

16. *Congressional Record,* 2 April 1964.
17. *Congressional Record,* 2 April 1964.

zations were also on the grounds early to distribute food and clothing and try to arrange housing. The Salvation Army and the American Red Cross were only two of a number of organizations that directed their attention to Alaska.

The discussions in the Senate indicated that there was no dissent on the issue of providing substantial help to Alaska. Aside from basic humanitarian feelings, other factors caused the government to spring to charitable tasks with alacrity. Senator Spessard Holland (D., Florida) gave two reasons for his belief that the fledgling state would not be finished by the devastating blow that nature had struck: "I have felt," he said, "that Alaska has become our last great frontier. The people there are pioneers of the finest possible stock, and I know they will rise superbly to this terrible emergency." Alaska was going to have assistance "in a very strong and powerful way, of this great nation." Holland's second reason for supporting the relief cause was a national one: "It may be that it requires an occasion of this kind, when the Nation is being torn somewhat by internal dissension, to make us realize that the collective strength of this great nation can mean much in helping to meet, as far as mens' means can meet, a terrible emergency of this kind." [18]

On September 30, Senator E. L. Bartlett rose to address the Senate on the earthquake and its aftermath. His address, printed in the *Congressional Record* and entitled "Americans Can Be Proud," was an eloquently delivered expression of gratitude. He first paid tribute to "the great spirit which on that terrible night moved Alaskans to unite and to begin the awesome task of reconstruction before the earth stopped moving under their feet," then went on to name all those who helped out. He singled out, among others, Edward A. McDermott, director of the Office of Emergency Planning, and Senator Clinton P. Anderson, whom President Johnson named to be chairman of a newly created Federal Reconstruction Commission, only a few days after the earthquake: "Their contributions have inspired and made possible the recovery of the forty-ninth state, a task which six months ago seemed almost insurmountable." [19]

The roll call of private individuals cited by Bartlett was im-

18. *Congressional Record,* 30 March 1964.
19. *Congressional Record,* 30 September 1964.

pressive. Employees of the International Telephone and Telegraph Corporation had given "thousands of dollars" to Valdez. Ham-radio operators all over the country helped relay Alaskan messages while the regular communications system was out of service. There was a seven-year-old boy who wrote the mayor of Anchorage: "I wanted to send my Easter basket but my daddy said the eggs would not last. I am sending you $1 instead." [20] There were the services provided by the YMCA, the American Council of Churches, Veterans of Foreign Wars, AFL-CIO, and many others.

The Federal Reconstruction Commission co-ordinated the necessary rebuilding. A measure of its success was the extent of recovery accomplished through a single spring and summer. Officials gave top priority to the restoration of water and sewer lines. Next came the damaged highways, the rails of the Alaska railroad; work on schools, airfields, and ports followed. Luckily, the major source of electric power, the Eklutna hydroelectric project, received only minor damage and, after being shut down for a few hours, functioned throughout the emergency. Houses and other structures were repaired or replaced at a fast pace.

All in all, it was a great effort. With some flourish, Senator Bartlett saluted all who had participated in the recovery. More work remained, but "the faith of so many was well planted. Alaska is on the way back." [21]

The earthquake occurrence and its aftermath serves as an excellent illustration of recurring themes in Alaska's history. The magnitude of the shock matched the physical vastness of the land. A charitable federal government rushed aid to the stricken region. And, of course, Alaskans and outsiders insisted that the spirit of the "last frontier" manifested itself during the emergency. Only one major link with the past was lacking: for once, Alaskans had nothing but praise for their national government.

20. *Congressional Record*, 30 September 1964.
21. *Congressional Record*, 30 September 1964.

12

Fury over the Resources

WHENEVER fans and foes of development have met head-on over some Alaskan issue, sound and fury has been certain. Vitriolic slander of opponents and passionate devotion to one's own cause were always present, whether the issues concerned pelagic sealing, salmon management, coal-land withdrawal, or railroad construction. The majority of Alaskans have favored development and have impugned the motives and sanity of those opposing it. The great national tide of conservation sentiment that arose in the 1960s affected Alaska as well as the rest of the country, and its people demonstrated that they, too, were concerned about their environment. Active conservationists were not numerous, but they had powerful allies Outside and could rely upon the emotions that had been aroused against projects threatening severe ecological change. The 1960s and 1970s saw three major battles over Alaskan issues, each encompassing several distinct aspects of the controversy over development and conservation. Although they did not always win, the voices for development predominated in each of these clashes: the Cape Thompson Atomic Energy Commission project, the Rampart Dam, and the Trans-Alaska pipeline.

Alaskans' near-paranoia over the action or inaction of federal agencies throughout the area's history may have been baseless at times, but the machinations of the Atomic Energy Commission in promoting Project Chariot, as the Cape Thompson project was called, justified the fears expressed. The agency wished to test an atomic bomb in the North, but chose to mask the test as a development project. "The Chariot story," wrote one critic, "is peculiarly disturbing as an illustration of the secrecy and cynicism (and initially also ignorance) with which a powerful government agency may work." [1]

In the spring of 1958, the AEC asked the U.S. Geological Survey about the geological and oceanographical features of the coast between Nome and Barrow. At the same time, it commissioned a private consulting firm to report on the mineral resources of the region. Neither report was based on field investigation. The USGS indicated that little was known of the region's geology, while the mineral report predicted that a port at Cape Thompson could handle the plentiful deposits of oil and coal in the region. That information seemed to encourage the AEC. The agency announced its plan to excavate a harbor at Cape Thompson. Extraction of the mineral wealth in that area had been retarded by lack of a harbor, and the AEC meant to fill a serious need. So that blasting could commence in 1960, the AEC requested a withdrawal of 1,600 square miles of land and water from the public domain.

Dr. Edward Teller, a Hungarian-born physicist, spearheaded the public-relations efforts for the AEC in Alaska. He insisted that Alaskans could choose the harbor site and that the entire operation would be suspended if it were not economically feasible. Yet, in fact, planners had already decided upon the site, and the agency apparently had planned no substantial economic study.

Some Alaskans protested against Chariot, as the project was called, and argued that it was unlikely that the creation of a harbor would foster a mining industry. There were many other factors that could prevent such a development—particularly the remoteness of the region and the very limited navigational season. At that point, the agency stopped talking about a harbor and began stressing the need to gather additional data on crater-producing nuclear detonations. The AEC let contracts to indi-

1. Paul Brooks, *The Pursuit of Wilderness* (Boston: Houghton Mifflin Co., 1971), p. 60.

viduals and scientific institutions for environmental studies of the Cape Thompson area.

As the environmental studies went on, some of the scientists became uneasy over recommendations emerging from the Environmental Committee to which they submitted their data. Why, they asked, did the committee recommend a blast in March and April, just as the AEC physicists had done earlier, when no study had yet been made of biological conditions in those months? The AEC gave no satisfactory answer to that question. To several scientists, it seemed clear that the Environmental Committee—supposedly composed of impartial scientists—was merely rubber-stamping predetermined AEC policies.

A University of Alaska biologist, Leslie Viereck, resigned from the project at that point. He insisted that the data collected by field investigators had been ignored when it conflicted with AEC plans. The committee chief had stated that Eskimos seldom hunted in the Cape Thompson area, but the committee's investigator of the hunting pattern, Don Foote, reported just the opposite. Viereck also noted that the AEC had stated publicly that all project biologists agreed that a detonation would not affect the environment adversely. Actually, the biologists were not in accord. Some believed that the test could be extremely hazardous.

Foote, Viereck, and others expressed to the Alaska Conservation Society their apprehension concerning the test and its effects on the Eskimos' food cycle. The Sierra Club also took up the cause and demanded that more investigation of blasting results be made. Its bulletin pointed out that no nuclear explosion had ever been detonated in a permanently frozen, mudstone geological formation; also, no series of simultaneous atomic blasts such as those planned for Chariot had ever taken place.

Foote corresponded with everyone who might respond to his calls of alarm. Caribou flesh commonly contained about seven times as much strontium 90 as the meat of domestic cattle. It was that peculiar susceptibility to radioactive fall-out that concerned Foote. Caribou subsisted on lichens that took their nutriment from dust carried down with rain and snow. Lichen thus absorbed radioactive fall-out before it became diluted in the soil. Eskimos ate caribou meat and took in a good deal of strontium 90. As the Point Hope Eskimos expressed it, in their letters to the president: "We also know about strontium 90, how it might harm people if too much of it gets into our body. . . . We are deeply concerned about the health of our people now and for the future." Alaska's Senator E. L. Bartlett became concerned about Project Chariot for another reason. He noted some confusion among AEC planners and wondered that anyone could believe that a harbor would attract private development. "If there is such absolute lack of co-ordination within the Commission in planning, goodness knows what would happen when the trigger were pulled. For one, I hope the AEC does its blasting elsewhere." [2]

Later, Bartlett asked the AEC whether it was true that some biologists working on Chariot disagreed with the AEC conclusions and planned to issue a minority report. An AEC official skirted Bartlett's query and stated that committee investigator Don Foote believed that the Project Chariot Environmental Committee had exceeded its authority. But the AEC wanted it understood "that of 85 investigators employed in these surveys, Mr. Foote is the only member to develop this extreme attitude." [3]

Most newspapers in Alaska rooted for Project Chariot. It would bring more federal money to the new state and attract worldwide attention. The *Fairbanks Daily News-Miner* editorialized that a huge nuclear blast in Alaska would be a fitting overture to the new era that was opening for the state.

The *Anchorage Daily Times* argued that the atomic explosion "is needed for [the] progress of man" and urged that it be carried forward as speedily as possible. The newspaper conceded that there had been some opposition based on ecological disturbance, condemned "premature judging of the project," and suggested that critics wait for the results of scientific studies. Prejudices would be a poor basis for any decision, the *Times* warned: "It would be better to approach the project with

2. Quoted in Brooks, *Pursuit of Wilderness*, pp. 63, 68.
3. "Project Chariot—The Long Look," *Sierra Club Bulletin*, May 1961, p. 6.

a favorable attitude." Man must progress. The use of dynamite would still be a mystery if man had not had the courage to experiment. "Nuclear power opens amazing new avenues for greater achievements, mankind must explore them and the Alaska experiment may be the key." [4]

Eskimos of Point Hope, a village of three hundred souls likely to be affected by the blast, were not in accord with the sentiments of Fairbanks and Anchorage publishers. They appealed to the governor, who assured them that there would be no test until he was convinced there would not be any harmful results. The Association of American Indians heard the Eskimos' pleas and sponsored the first general meeting ever held by Alaskan Eskimos. That meeting of village representatives at Barrow attracted much publicity to the Eskimo protest, and it was an extremely important step in developing the co-operation and self-awareness necessary in the later struggle for settlement of aboriginal claims.

The Eskimos' deliberations in November 1961 resulted in a report that commenced with an expression of their fears. "We the Inupiat have come together for the first time ever in all the years of our history. We had to come together in meeting from our far villages from Lower Kuskokwim to Point Barrow. We had to come from so far together for this reason. We always thought our Inupiat Paitot [aboriginal hunting rights] was safe to be passed down to our future generations as our fathers passed it down to us. Our Inupiat Paitot is our land around the whole Arctic world where the Inupiat live." [5]

Eskimo protests against the blast began in 1959, and in 1961 villagers wrote to the president of their concern: "All the four seasons, each month, we get what we need for living. In December, January, February, and even March we get the polar bear, seals, tomcod, oogrook, walrus, fox, and caribou. In March we also get crabs. In April, May, and June, we hunt whales, ducks, seals, white beluga, and oogrook. In July we collect crowbell eggs from Cape Thompson. . . . The ice we

4. *Anchorage Daily Times,* editorial, June 29, 1961.

5. Quoted in Brooks, *Pursuit of Wilderness,* p. 73.

get for our drinking water during the winter is about twelve miles off from our village towards Cape Thompson.'' [6]

The effect of an atomic explosion on the sea cliffs north of Cape Thompson was a matter of prime concern. Thousands of seabirds—murres, guillemots, puffins, gulls, kittiwakes, and others—nested there. Eskimos gathered their eggs for food, which would be lost if the cliffs were destroyed.

It was August 1962 before the AEC announced a change of plans: Project Chariot was to be shelved. No reasons were given. Neither Don Foote nor the conservationists were mentioned, and the agency continued to insist that its studies indicated no danger to the inhabitants of the area or to fish or wildlife from the proposed blast. The AEC had spent $3 million on the project before giving up.

The AEC did do some blasting in Alaska at underground sites on Amchitka Island in the Aleutians. Tests were conducted in 1965, 1969, and 1971, and the chorus of protest against them was vigorous within and outside Alaska each time. There were no people living within hundreds of miles of the explosions on Amchitka Island, so the situation differed from that of Project Chariot. The test results were monitored closely, and more than a million dollars was expended to restore the island ecologically to its state prior to the blasts. One new geographical feature created by the 1971 explosion of a bomb buried nearly six thousand feet under the ground is a lake fifty-five feet deep and one and a half miles across. Wildlife is returning to the island, but the U.S. Bureau of Sports Fisheries and Wildlife predicts that it will take years before the animal numbers reach their preblast level.

Protests against the Amchitka tests may have helped deter the agency from continuing their experiments. In December 1973, the AEC announced that no more tests would be conducted on Amchitka.

Project Chariot and the Amchitka tests offer significant examples of the curious relationship between Alaska and the rest of the nation. As with so many other matters that have affected Alaskans, Washington decided to use the region as a testing

6. Quoted in Brooks, *Pursuit of Wilderness*, p. 63.

ground without consulting Alaskans themselves. The AEC offered Project Chariot as an aid to economic development because that approach had always been a popular one. But many Americans expressed a good deal of opposition to all of the tests. Once again, battle lines were sharply drawn between those who feared that Alaska was being exploited and those wishing to make some use of the land and its resources.

In the 1960s, another major conflict over land use arose over a dam proposed for the middle Yukon River. The dam was the pet project of Alaska's U.S. Senator Ernest Gruening, but it was stubbornly opposed by a coalition of conservationists and Alaskan natives.

The battle started after a study by the U.S. Army Corps of Engineers indicated the feasibility of constructing a dam at a narrow portion of the middle Yukon River, near the settlement of Rampart, about a hundred miles northwest of Fairbanks. Statistics cited for the huge project were impressive. An area of ten thousand square miles would have to be flooded to provide a reservoir that would be 10 percent larger than Lake Erie and require some eighteen years to fill. Five million kilowatts of power would be generated each year. The construction cost would be $1.3 billion. The proposed Rampart Dam would be the largest dam in the world, generating two and a half times as much power as Grand Coulee and twice that of any other dam in existence. According to its promoters, the benefits of the dam would be abundant. Most of Alaska's businessmen, labor leaders, and politicians rallied to the cause. Much was made of the huge construction payrolls, and in a region that had become accustomed to a heavy dependence on federal military construction projects, that was a potent factor. Under those circumstances, who would dare shout the horrid word *boondoggle?* As a matter of fact, many taxpayers in and out of Alaska did just that. The need for cheap hydroelectric power in interior Alaska, where no manufacturing industry existed, did not seem compelling to all. Nor was it clear that the conveyance of the energy elsewhere would be practical because of the loss of energy that would occur in transmission.

Alaska's Senator Ernest Gruening led the fight for the dam.

Gruening was a tough political warrior who had long been identified with liberal causes. Earlier in his career, he had been a
crusading editor of *The Nation,* had championed the cause of
Latin Americans against exploitive American interests, had
fought long and hard for birth-control measures, and had pushed
tax reform through Alaska's legislature over the outraged protests of business interests. In addition, he earned the gratitude of
many by his unrelenting protest of the nation's Vietnam war
participation. In the U.S. Senate, only Gruening and Wayne
Morse voted against the Tonkin Gulf Resolution. With such a
record as that, Gruening could be forgiven for assuming that his
objective attitude toward commerce had been clearly established
through hard-fought battles. And, like most men of spirit, conviction, and ego, he was understandably appalled when some
Alaskans would not accept his blessing of the construction of
Rampart Dam. Gruening was too wise and too big a man to
declare that he knew best; but in his stubborn, fierce advocacy,
he showed very clearly that he believed it.

Members of the small Alaska Conservation Society worked
desperately to create opposition to the dam. At times, their
cause must have seemed hopeless. Alaska's leading newspapers
editorialized in support of Rampart, and civic leaders put up
money for propaganda. The Yukon Power for America organization was formed, and it produced an attractive brochure defining the marvels of the dam. State legislators introduced bills
calling for an appropriation for prodam publicity and passed a
resolution calling for the federal government to get moving on
construction. But during the 1964 session of the state legislature, Senator Jay Hammond co-sponsored a resolution against
the use of state funds for promotion of federal action prior to the
completion of government studies of the project. Hammond had
indicated his position as early as January 1962, in a report for
the Conservation Society's newsletter, which cast doubt on
some of the dam proponents' arguments. Hammond also noted
that Senator Gruening had placed in the *Congressional Record* a
resolution of the Alaska Senate that had not passed in the form
quoted. The original resolution, which had not passed, urged
construction; the amended version that finally passed urged

prompt environmental studies. Hammond did not belabor the obvious differences between the two resolutions, but it was clear that Gruening had indulged in a bit of artful deceit.

Alaskan conservationists had other powerful friends, as well. National conservation groups gave support, and associations of sportsmen were zealous foes of the dam, once they had been alerted to the alleged detrimental effects on waterfowl. The Wildlife Management Institute warned members that "Rampart Dam is synonymous with resource destruction." [7] The potential use of Rampart power was uncertain, but it was clear that the wetlands to be flooded supported one and a half million ducks, geese, swans, and cranes.

Conservationists were elated when officials of a federal agency—the Fish and Wildlife Service—announced publicly that the Yukon salmon's spawning ground would be endangered by dam construction. Gruening tried to keep the Fish and Wildlife men from raising objections in the press. His complaints to Secretary of the Interior Stewart Udall were ineffective, however. Udall was known to favor parks and recreation projects over dam construction.

The conservationists refuted Gruening's insistence that the issue was simply that of the competing needs of birds and people. They did not oppose economic development in itself, but feared the adverse changes, for wildlife and people, that might occur in the entire Yukon basin. They also pointed out that too much was claimed for the dam. Promotional literature exclaimed that Rampart would provide the key to unlocking Alaska's long-buried treasures. "The reservoir itself would 'open vast areas to mineral and timber development,' and provide unlimited recreational potential." [8]

Gruening struck hard at the position of the Wildlife Management Institute on several counts. He charged that its director, Ira Gabrielson, as former director of the federal Fish and Wildlife Service, had presided over the depletion of Alaska's salmon, "the gravest conservation disaster since game and fishery management had come to be recognized procedures." Also, Ga-

7. Gruening, *Many Battles*, p. 498.
8. Brooks, *Pursuit of Wilderness*, p. 79.

brielson had opposed oil development on the Kenai Peninsula and had prophesied that the moose of the region would be lost— which did not turn out to be true. Then Gruening launched his heaviest barrage: "Finally, without impugning Gabrielson's devotion to the abstraction which he was unable to materialize in practice," the Wildlife Management Institute was financed by gun-makers and ammunition manufacturers. Gruening did not think gun-makers provided disinterested opinion. "Was preserving the ducks in Alaska so they could be blasted from the skies in the states really a praiseworthy demonstration of conservation?" [9]

Conservationists expressed particular indignation at the often-quoted question posed by Rampart Dam proponents: "Who ever heard of a duck drowning?" That was indicative of a frivolous disregard for the serious issues, they felt. But Gruening was just as angry at an article written by Paul Brooks and published in the *Atlantic*. The title was provocative—"The Plot to Drown Alaska"—and one photograph showed a swimming moose, "a sight familiar to Alaskans but which implied to the uninformed that the poor animal was drowning." [10]

Each side accused the other of disregarding the human residents of the Yukon flats. Gruening felt that the relocation of seven small Indian villages of the Yukon flats would be of economic and aesthetic advantage to them. Conservationists were equally sure that the relocation would be an unwarranted interference with a traditional subsistence pattern of life that deserved preservation. Both advocates claimed support from the natives for their views on the question, and neither believed that the other actually cared what happened to the human residents. Gruening, a skilled protagonist, made much of another point on the humanistic side: the conservationists were callous to the needs of all Alaskans and all Americans for a reliable supply of energy.

The case was finally resolved in 1965. Secretary Udall recommended against the building of Rampart, and Congress refused to support the project. The conservationists were happy

9. Gruening, *Many Battles*, p. 498.
10. Gruening, *Many Battles*, p. 499.

and relieved to discover that their cause had been supported Outside. They had learned a good deal and, a few years later, were to take on another threat: the Trans-Alaskan pipeline. In the pipeline conflict, there were different alignments of pressure groups, and issues were very complex. Still, it was clearly a familiar struggle of conservationists versus developers and, even less than in earlier contests, the determining factors arose out of conditions that were only peripheral to considerations of Alaska's environment.

Years after the dam project had been defeated, Gruening was still miffed at the obduracy of the Alaskans who contested it. In his autobiography, *Many Battles,* the senator recalled the "extreme opposition" he encountered, summarized his arguments in favor of the dam, and defended his credentials as a conservationist: "I am on the side of the concerned environmentalist and consider myself not only a conservationist but a fervent one." He disagreed with "some of my fellow conservationists, whom I class as extremists," because they put ducks before people.[11]

There is no such thing as a last word on conservation debates, yet Gruening expressed himself graciously in praising the efforts of his Rampart antagonists: "They are campaigning against the human greed and stupidity which have so tragically destroyed much of our environment and may threaten men's very survival on our small planet." But he warned, "sometimes these friends of nature are, in their laudable zeal, misguided, too." [12] That is the crux of the issue, of course. Who are the true friends of nature? How do we know when their warnings are plausible? How do we distinguish the fanatics from the selfish? All we can be sure of is that there will be other rounds in the contest.

The most recent major struggle over land use coincided with the decision of the petroleum industry to develop the resources of the North Slope. Atlantic-Richfield made its momentous discovery at Prudhoe Bay on Alaska's Arctic coast in 1968 and announced its plans to join other interested petroleum companies in bringing the Arctic field into production. Transportation of the product was a major consideration. The industry formed a

11. Gruening, *Many Battles,* p. 500.
12. Gruening, *Many Battles,* p. 500.

consortium, initially called the Trans-Alaska Pipeline and later reorganized as the Alyeska Pipeline Company. Alyeska would undertake the construction of a pipeline from Prudhoe Bay to the port of Valdez, a terminal at Valdez, and all the pumping stations, camps, bridges, and roads necessary to support the project.

Alyeska hopes to complete its work and have oil flowing by 1977. The pipeline is an ambitious undertaking, a line of forty-eight-inch pipe stretching for 798 miles from sea level, at Prudhoe, to a 4,800-foot pass in the Brooks Range, then going on to span thirty-four major rivers and streams and finally passing over a 3,500-foot pass through the Alaska Range before descending to Valdez. Projected costs continue to escalate, but at this writing Alyeska expects to spend $8 billion on the job—which makes the pipeline the most expensive project ever undertaken by American private industry anywhere.

The scope of the pipeline construction concerned environmentalists. The Sierra Club and other conservationist groups had been urging the formation of a Gates-of-the-Arctic National Park in the Brooks Range, and now it appeared that the whole region might be devastated by construction and oil spills.

Few Americans have ever seen the Brooks Range, but the region has had eloquent champions. The most notable was Robert Marshall, a naturalist and a perceptive writer, who wrote about his sojourn in the settlement of Wiseman in his book *Arctic Village*. More than forty years ago, Marshall called for the conservation of the wilderness: "There is just one hope of repulsing the tyrannical ambition of civilization to conquer every niche on the whole earth. That hope is the organization of spirited people who will fight for the freedom of the wilderness." In 1969, these strong voices on behalf of conservation were yet needed. At that time, Samuel A. Wright, a biologist who spent two winters—1969 and 1970—in an isolated cabin in the Brooks Range explained his notion of the wilderness and his motivation for living in it: "We have chosen to live in this last great wilderness, disturbing it as little as possible and becoming a part of its ecology." He considered his reason to be an important one: "One reason for this choice was the recognition that at this moment in history this great wilderness is doomed unless voices speak out in its behalf. And, certainly a voice should come from the wilderness itself." [13]

Conservationists geared up in the late 1960s, realizing that it was now or never. If they could not halt the juggernaut of petroleum development at once, it would soon be too far advanced to be resisted. Their basic argument was presented endlessly: oil development would destroy the natural beauty of the state, pollute its rivers and oceans, and cause devastating, irrevocable harm to the fragile ecology. For those, mostly Alaskans, who did not respond to the wilderness theme, the conservationists staunchly presented economic theories. "For Alaskans, wilderness can also be a great economic asset. If tapped, the oil will be exhausted, even as gold was. Protected wilderness, on the other hand, can remain forever as an increasingly attractive resource that will bring hundreds of thousands of people and, with them, millions of dollars to the state of Alaska." The writer was certain of his position. "This is an infinite resource—perpetual money in the bank." [14]

In *Oil on Ice,* a recent publication of the Sierra Club, biologist Wright warned again that "there is no time left. . . . We must preserve any wilderness left on this planet that we have now seen from the moon to be our home, or the opportunity is lost forever." He argued that Alaskans erred in believing they could have economic development of a scale paralleling that of the North Slope scale and still maintain an unmutilated natural environment. The cocksureness of developers frightened the author of *Oil on Ice,* and he quoted a state official who supposedly said: "Hell, this country's so goddam big that even if industry went wild we could never wreck it. We can have our cake and eat it too." [15]

But the governor and legislators in Juneau went ahead with leasing plans, despite such pleas as those uttered in *Oil on Ice.*

13. George Marshall, "Introduction to the Second Edition," in Robert Marshall's *Alaska Wilderness* (Berkeley: University of California Press, 1970), pp. xix, xx, xxi.

14. Edgar Wayburn, "Afterword," in Tom Brown's *Oil on Ice: Alaskan Wilderness at the Crossroads* (San Francisco, New York: Sierra Club Books, 1971), pp. 151–152.

15. Samuel A. Wright and Henry Pratt, quoted in Brown, *Oil on Ice,* pp. 8, 9.

Everything will be fine, they insisted; the state will impose strict controls; there will be no oil spills on land or sea; yes, the Hickel Highway, a crude, winter-haul road that was gashed through from Fairbanks to Prudhoe Bay in 1969–1970 was an unfortunate slip-up—but we learned from that mishap—let's get rolling, so that we can meet the state's urgent social and economic needs.

Conservationists put up a spirited battle to halt the construction of the pipeline from Prudhoe Bay to Valdez. The pipeline was correctly seen as the key to the development of the North Slope. If its construction could be prevented, there were no other means by which North Slope petroleum could be brought to market. The trial voyage of the huge icebreaking tanker *Manhattan* to Prudhoe Bay in 1970 demonstrated that it was technically possible to haul oil by ship, but it also indicated that such a route was not economically profitable.

The conservationists tested the rigors of the new federal Environmental Protection Act, which stipulated that the environmental impact of all construction and development be determined before the Secretary of the Interior could grant a permit of approval for development projects. Opponents of the pipeline were supported by the courts in their endeavor to show that neither the state nor the oil companies had a very clear picture of what impact the pipeline would have on the land.

At hearings in Washington, Anchorage, Fairbanks, and elsewhere, all parties received a fair hearing, an opportunity to present their views. Oil company executives writhed in anguish at the prospect of losing the millions of dollars that had already been tied up in leases and equipment and protested that further delays would greatly accelerate the cost of construction. But a cooler assessment of the situation prevailed, and studies of the environment that should have been made earlier were undertaken. The oil industry was pained over the delay in construction. Such agonizing over the ecological effects of construction departed from American tradition, the oil executives said. "Let her rip!" had traditionally been the cry; but Americans were sick of what had happened to their air, water, and natural surroundings in the late 1960s. The reaction led to the passage of the Environmental Protection Act.

State officials also suffered, during the postponement of construction during the first 'half of the 1970s. Mournfully, the Alaska Commissioner of Labor told U.S. Department of Interior officials about Alaska's chronically high rate of unemployment. In February 1971, he said, about 15 percent of the labor force would be unemployed. "Public officials concerned with human beings will have little patience with the witless and heartless recommendations that the permit be delayed for one year or five years or for a generation," the commissioner warned. He went on to "make bold to suggest that the effects on the people in this state and their future are even more important than stream siltation, interruptions of migratory paths of caribou, changed habitat zones and the aesthetics of this ribbon of steel crossing unoccupied wastes of the Arctic tundra." [16]

Alaska's Commissioner of the Department of Health and Welfare also stressed the human suffering that would result from a further delay in construction. Programs for welfare, old-age assistance, medical aid, and education would all be severely curtailed if anticipated oil revenue were not realized. He also stressed the state's ability to insure that the land was protected from ravages caused by construction or oil spills: "The state of Alaska is prepared by present and proposed arrangements to monitor a project of this magnitude." Through co-operative effort with other state and federal agencies, "we have developed a strong program which exhibits our common concern for environmental protection." [17]

Alaskan newspapers reacted angrily to the testimony of conservationists at the hearings. "There isn't much the Interior Department can do or say that will convince the new environmental crusaders the pipeline is not going to be a catastrophe," wrote a Ketchikan editor, noting the cranks in the country "who

16. U.S., Department of the Interior, *Draft, Environmental Impact Statement for the Trans-Alaskan Pipeline* (Washington, D.C.: Government Printing Office, 1971), 1, Exhibit 12:2, 3.

17. U.S., Interior, *Environmental Impact Statement,* Exhibit 13:4.

are not interested in a pipeline under any conditions and they add their voices to professional conservationists who make a practice of opposing any development any place—Sierra Club, Friends of the Earth, etc." Why should some people assume that eight hundred miles of pipeline laid across an area one-fifth the size of the United States would cause a natural disaster when so many pipelines crisscross the states? "From the terrible predictions we have heard . . . we should expect to find the lower 48 with its 217,000 miles of oil pipelines up to its ears in oil." [18]

Pressures mounted on the Interior Department from all quarters as the permit delay continued. The Secretary announced several times that he felt the permit would surely be issued, but that more information was needed from the oil companies. Then, in 1970, in the midst of all the pleading and wrangling, a crisis arose with the major suppliers of the world's petroleum. Middle Eastern oil-producing countries flexed their muscles, cut down on exports, and jacked up their prices. For the first time since World War II, gas for cars and heating oil for homes was in short supply in the United States. There was much debate over the legitimacy of the crisis, but the general panic of the American public and Congress was honest enough. Now the environmental issue did not seem so critical; and the case of the conservationists, no matter how rational it may have been, did not have its former emotional impact. The president of the United States called for speedy issuance of a permit, and Congress agreed that an emergency prevailed that made pipeline construction a matter of national priority. Futile efforts were made to hold the project up in the courts after Congress acted, but the judiciary could find no further grounds to sustain a delay.

Construction began in 1973, as an army of workers—more than twenty thousand at peak times—signed on with Alyeska. The company dispatched men and women to Arctic camps at Prudhoe, Wiseman, Coldfoot, and elsewhere, and to other instant modular camps in Fairbanks, Delta, and along the southern

18. *Ketchikan Daily News*, February 18, 1971.

end of the transportation corridor. The work proceeded at a good pace. In the summer of 1974, the road north of Livengood to Prudhoe was pushed through; and the next summer, the first bridge ever built over the Yukon River in Alaska was completed. At this writing, the biggest private construction project in history is on schedule, and the Arctic region and the Yukon valley, once populated by only scattered Eskimo and Indian settlements and containing much wildlife, now hums with building activity.

13

This Land Is Ours

*T*HE original charter of the Russian American Company contained no provisions covering the status of the natives of Alaska or the land used and inhabited by them. It merely provided that "the principal object of the Company being the catching of sea animals and wild beasts, the Company has no need to spread its rule from the coast where it practices its catchings, into the interior of the country, and it should not make efforts to conquer tribes inhabiting these coasts." That prohibition of conquest was repeated in the 1844 charter: "The colonial government shall not forcibly extend the possession of the Company in regions inhabited by tribes not dependent on the colonial authorities." [1]

In the 1867 treaty of purchase, Russian and American diplomats recognized the differences among natives. Some had mixed blood and resided in communities like Sitka. Others were wholly independent of the company. Thus the treaty stipulated that Alaskans could choose to become American citizens, but "with the exception of uncivilized native tribes." The uncivilized natives "will be subject to such laws and regulations as the United States may, from time to time, adopt in regard to aboriginal tribes of that country." [2]

1. U.S., Congress, Senate, *Alaska Native Claims Settlement Act of 1971, Report to Accompany S. 34,* 92d Cong., 1st sess., 1971, Senate Rept. No. 405, p. 88.
2. *Native Claims Settlement,* p. 89.

The foundations of the American policy toward native land claims were laid in the Northwest Ordinance of 1788: "The utmost good faith shall always be observed towards the Indians, their lands and property shall never be taken from them without consent: and in their property rights and liberty they never shall be invaded or disturbed, unless in just and lawful wars authorized by Congress." [3]

Congress ignored Alaska until the Organic Act of 1884, which designated the territory a land district, extended the mining laws of the United States, and provided:

> That the Indians or other persons in said districts shall not be disturbed in the possession of any lands actually in their use or occupation or now claimed by them but the terms under which such persons may acquire title to such lands is reserved from future legislation by Congress. [4]

The phrase "or now claimed by them" was added deliberately by the legislators. They realized that they knew little about Alaska and desired "that the Indian shall at least have as many rights after the passage of this bill as he had before." [5]

In 1884, no reservations existed in Alaska. Generally, reservations came into being as a result of treaties between natives and whites, but the government had never made a treaty with any Alaskan natives. Congress did act in 1891 to create a reservation of 86,000 acres on Annette Island "for the use of the Metlakahtla Indians . . . who recently immigrated from British Columbia to Alaska." [6]

The great influx of gold-rushers in 1898 somewhat jolted the government's indifference to natives' land claims. The impact of stampeders on the Tlingits of southeastern Alaska was particularly severe, and the Indians there appealed to Territorial Governor John Brady for help. Their complaints could not be easily reconciled. They admitted to an admiration for the whites' culture, yet demanded protection for their traditional hunting and fishing subsistence pattern.

3. *Native Claims Settlement*, p. 88.
4. *Native Claims Settlement*, p. 89.
5. *Native Claims Settlement*, p. 89.
6. *Native Claims Settlement*, p. 90.

"We have places where we used to trap furs; now the white man get up on these grounds," said a chief from Wrangell to Brady. Whites were getting much gold money. "Here at this place as well as other places they take our property, take away ground, and when we complain to them about it, they employ a lawyer and go to court and win the case." Indians wished Brady to write to Washington where the Big Chief resided. "We also ask him to return our creeks and the hunting grounds that white people have taken away from us." [7]

Another chief affirmed his willingness to give the country to the whites, although insisting that "we know this is our country." But he pointed out that Alaskan Indians had not given any trouble, as had Indians elsewhere, and they thought they should be given back "the places that brought us food." [8]

A third Indian petitioner was most articulate. He had once traveled to Seattle and Tacoma and thought those were nice towns. He was sure that he would not be allowed to destroy the gardens he had observed there. By the same token, whites should give back the places where Indians fished, trapped, and hunted. "And if white men should like to take possession of any of those places, we should like to ask you to tell them to not take them for nothing, but to pay for them." [9]

The Indians wanted the government to keep better order among the people. All knew that liquor was the source of the trouble. "Some of my people do not behave themselves, especially on Christmas, and will get to fighting," one said. "They get clubs and sticks and strike each other with clubs and some strike with knives. I want that to be stopped." [10]

Brady responded to the chiefs at some length. He argued that the Russians had treated them as savages who could not be trusted, but that the United States "has treated them kindly and proposes to treat them well." [11] Tlingits had not always been

7. Ted C. Hinckley, editor, "The Canoe Rocks—We Do Not Know What Will Become of Us," *Western Historical Quarterly* 1 (July 1970):271.

8. Hinckley, "The Canoe Rocks," p. 273.

9. Hinckley, "The Canoe Rocks," p. 276.

10. Hinckley, "The Canoe Rocks," p. 279.

11. Hinckley, "The Canoe Rocks," p. 284.

good, he reminded them, and the Russians had reasons for fearing them.

But the governor refused to accept the Indians' image of themselves as oppressed, downtrodden victims of white encroachment. Things had improved for the Tlingits, Brady argued. Earlier they owned few shoes or blankets and had fought among themselves constantly. "I know that the Tlingit are better off today than they ever were before in their lives," [12] he stated, pointing out that in Sitka there was one hundred dollars for every fifty cents Indians had had earlier.

Brady admitted that the Organic Act of 1884 guaranteed that Indians should not be disturbed in their possession of land, and he assured them that the law would be adhered to. He remained somewhat vague on the meaning of the law, but seemed certain that the Indians could not claim the whole district. "The question is, do you wish to be put on an island and not abandon your old customs? Do you wish to be citizens of the United States and have their protection? It is for you to say." Brady suggested that they might want to move to Admiralty Island to live by themselves "and not be disturbed and have agents over them to keep them straight." The alternative was to obey white man's laws and have all his privileges. "Which do you want?" [13]

Brady closed his address on a stern note: Don't tell me you are poor and can't earn a living in this country; show some pride; see that your people do not sell their young daughters to miners as happened so often. Indians could work in canneries, Brady scolded, but they "persist in getting drunk" so the salmon packers had to ship in Chinese to do the work. [14]

Another government official declared in the closing remarks of the meeting that Tlingits were the equal of whites if they chose to be educated. "You must think of yourselves," he said, "and decide whether you want to be American citizens or want to live in your old customs." [15]

Congress enacted the Alaska Native Allotment Act in 1906.

12. Hinckley, "The Canoe Rocks," p. 284.
13. Hinckley, "The Canoe Rocks," p. 286.
14. Hinckley, "The Canoe Rocks," p. 287.
15. Hinckley, "The Canoe Rocks," p. 289.

The act represented the government's first attempt to deal with the natives' land status. Earlier legislation, such as the 1898 act extending homestead laws to Alaska, seemed to be preserving native rights. In the Homestead Act, tracts of land along the waterfront of any stream or bay had been reserved for "landing places for canoes and other craft used by natives." [16]

The Alaska Native Allotment Act appeared retrogressive—if not actually oppressive. It gave legal title to some lands occupied by natives and provided for the allotment of 160-acre homesteads for native heads of households. Natives did not understand the law, and few homesteads were taken up. Only eighty allotments were issued under the act in a half-century after its passage. Since the act contained no reference to the general rights of natives to the land, they could only hold possession against others through civil action. Yet, effectively, the courts were inaccessible to them because of distance, expense, and lack of knowledge.

A conference between government officials in 1915 shows how confused the land question remained. Alaska congressional delegate James Wickersham and other officials met with the Tanana chiefs. The Athabascans, like the Tlingits, wanted help and reminded Wickersham that Alaska had belonged to them before the whites came.

Wickersham offered two proposals: either the Indians could have a reservation selected, or they could each claim 160 acres of land under the Homestead Act. "If you don't do something," he warned, "the white man will take all the best land for theirs." [17]

A chief replied: "We don't want to go on a reservation, but wish to stay perfectly free just as we are now, and go about just the same as now, and believe that a reservation will not be a benefit to us." [18] What the Indians agreed upon was the need to have their villages and surrounding land protected from white encroachment.

16. *Native Claims Settlement,* p. 90.
17. Stanton H. Patty, "A Conference with the Tanana Chiefs," *Alaska Journal,* Spring 1971, p. 5.
18. Patty, "Conference with Tanana Chiefs," p. 7.

Territorial Governor Thomas Riggs, Jr., assured the chiefs that their villages would be protected; but Wickersham, while insisting that the reservation scheme would not be pressed upon them, pushed hard for the Indians' acceptance of it. He realized that when the Indians asked for protection of their lands from whites, they were not thinking of just village sites, but of all the vast region they hunted and fished. "I don't agree with the people here," Wickersham said. "They think that a reservation is a bad thing. I think a reservation is excellent and the best thing that can be done for Indians." [19] Wickersham's arguments did not prevail. The chiefs decided to ask for homesteads, rather than a reservation.

The next issue discussed was the need for industrial schools. The Indians wished to learn trades to better their condition. Wickersham was all for their ambitions. He promised to convey their requests to the U.S. Secretary of the Interior. "He will read about them wanting schools and work, and that they want to make their homes and become like white people, and want to learn to talk the white man's language and to work like white man." [20] As soon as you establish homes and live like white men, Wickersham assured them, you can have the right to vote.

Wickersham did try to convince the Department of the Interior and the Congress that some kind of land settlement should be made. But the issue was so complex that Congress dodged it for years.

Other legislation subsequent to the Alaska Native Allotment Act of 1906 authorized the president to withdraw land for native reservations, and several such withdrawals were made. But in the language of the 1924 Citizenship Act, Congress seemed again to recognize the rights of natives to the land. The Act declared "that all noncitizen Indians born within the territorial limits of the United States be, and they are hereby, declared to be citizens of the United States: PROVIDED that the granting of such citizenship shall not in any manner impair or otherwise affect the right of any Indian to tribal or other property." [21]

19. Patty, "Conference with Tanana Chiefs," p. 11.
20. Patty, "Conference with Tanana Chiefs," p. 18.
21. *Native Claims Settlements,* p. 91.

In the 1940s several reservations were established by virtue of the Indian Reorganization Act of 1934 and its 1936 extension to Alaska. These reservations included Unalakleet, Akutan, Venetie, Karluk, Wales, and Little Diomede. But the single most critical recognition of native claims occurred in 1935 when Congress passed the Tlingit and Haida legislation that gave Indians of the Panhandle the right to bring suit in the U.S. Court of Claims. The law specified that Indians could ask for compensation for all land taken from them from 1867 to the present. The court must determine an equitable and just value for the loss to Indians "of their rights, title, or interest, arising from occupancy and use, in lands or other tribal or community property." [22] Congressional action finally gave natives an effective wedge, particularly since virtually all of southeastern Alaska had been withdrawn for national forests and closed to public use.

Judicial consideration of the Tlingit-Haida claims dragged on for years. Finally, in 1968, the court entered judgment in favor of the Indians for $7,546,053. The court also decreed that, except for eight small parcels for which patents had been granted, Indian title to an area of 2,634,744 acres had not been extinguished.

But the government refused to allow other natives to bring suit in the U.S. Court of Claims. A further blow to the natives had fallen when the Supreme Court had declared in 1955 that their land rights were not protected by the Fifth Amendment. With the coming of Alaskan statehood, the natives' land settlement hopes descended to a new low. The state's right to selection of 103 million acres threatened to bar the natives from all of the most valuable tracts available. In the ten years after statehood, 1959–1969, the state had selected 19 million acres. At the same time, Alaska's natives owned less than five hundred acres in fee simple and held restricted title to only fifteen thousand acres. Nine hundred native families lived on reserves which comprised 4 million acres. In these circumstances, the natives protested the state's land selection. Secretary of the Interior

22. *Native Claims Settlement,* p. 92.

Stewart Udall responded to the dispute by ordering a freeze on all land transfers in 1966. By 1968, various villages had recorded protests on some 296.6 million acres.

In a 1962 meeting of the Tanana chiefs—the first held since their complaints to Wickersham were stimulated because of the state's land selection—the complaints voiced were the familiar ones recorded at the conference with Wickersham and, in the previous century, at the meeting of Tlingits with Territorial Governor Brady, and other such meetings. The participants demanded land and educational opportunity.

"We are no longer secure on the land which had been ours for centuries," the chiefs stated. "New laws make it hard for us to hunt for food when we need it. We must buy food and there are not enough jobs for our people." When they had last met, the chiefs recalled, inaccurately, "the people had homes and meat and land. They were happy." [23]

But conditions had worsened in the half-century since they had last conferred. The white population had increased a good deal, particularly after World War II, and heavier pressure on the land resulted. *"Everywhere you turn you are bumping into a white man,"* cried the Minto chief. Statehood might have benefited whites, but it made things worse for Indians. "Now a man can only own land where his house is. The state is taking land right at Minto. If they take the land, our whole villages will have to move. *We do not want to move."* [24]

The Tanacross chief argued that the new state government was pernicious: "The state is taking advantage of the native people in Alaska." He issued a call for collective action. It was the same call that was echoing among Indians, Eskimos, and Aleuts all over the state: "We must get together and do something. There must be a way. We should have our land and build up our resources." [25]

The federal government was also blamed for disrupting natives' traditional use of the land. The army had taken land near Copper Center for recreational purposes with the Indians' ap-

23. *Report of Chiefs' Conference,* Fairbanks, June 24–26, 1962, p. 1.
24. *Chiefs' Conference,* p. 2.
25. *Chiefs' Conference,* p. 2.

proval, and now there were privately operated lodges all over the area. And the Fort Yukon chief had much to say about the threat of a huge federal project then in the offing—the proposed Rampart Dam: "Rampart Dam will flood our land, destroy our hunting, destroy our economy. We have lived for centuries in this Yukon Flat and do not want to be driven away." [26]

Three major recommendations were made by the Tanana chiefs. In clarity they were a far cry from the confused expressions of need that had issued from earlier grievance meetings. Clearly, the natives of Alaska had gained in education and political maturity since the Wickersham meeting. Their major requests:

1. We the Indians of the Athabascan villages join the Inupiat in their request that the Interior Department immediately withdraw from the public domain in Alaska tracts of land around all Native villages, pending the establishment of reservations for those which want them or other settlement of Alaska Native claims which also will give the Natives full land, hunting and mineral rights.
2. All villages should be truthfully informed how aboriginal land and hunting rights can be protected by the Interior Department without restricting the Natives' freedom as citizens; and all villages which wish to do so should be allowed to apply for a reservation with full mineral and hunting rights.
3. In the absence of any determination or litigation of the Congress of the United States, relative to the lands in question, and in the absence of definitive instruction of the Congress of the United States; we submit that the rentals and royalties, primarily to oil and gas, should be held in escrow pending the determination by Congress, or the courts.[27]

Interior Department and other federal officials mulled over the claims issue often. The Bureau of Indian Affairs argued that all the lands and waters that natives had hunted or fished should be reserved to them. The Bureau of Land Management pointed out that many natives lived in the same manner as whites and argued that a huge grant of land was an unreasonable solution to the claims dilemma.

26. *Chiefs' Conference*, p. 2.
27. *Chiefs' Conference*, p. 5.

Congress finally turned its attention to the land-claims issue in the late 1960s. The Interior Committee worked over several sessions on various claims bills. Petroleum interests favored a major land settlement in order to expedite the Prudhoe Bay-Valdez pipeline. Natives of Stevens Village had threatened to enjoin construction in their region, and other delays could be foreseen if the claims could not be settled satisfactorily.

Congressional hearings indicated a clear intent to treat natives with generosity. A report issued by the Committee on Interior and Insular Affairs stressed the contrast between whites and natives in standards of living. "Eskimos, Indians, and Aleuts spring from cultures very different from those of other Alaskans," it was noted. Most natives lived in widely scattered settlements and subsisted by fishing and hunting. Many natives were unemployed or only seasonally employed. "The bulk of them live in dire poverty—the poorest of America's poor." [28]

The Senate learned that seven out of ten adult natives had less than an elementary school education, and only one of ten natives graduated from high school. Children in small villages had to leave their homes for nine months a year to attend boarding schools.

Natives suffered poor health. "Largely because they lack cash income and because the costs of purchased goods and services are high, most natives live in small, dilapidated or substandard houses under unsanitary conditions." [29] Partly as a result of these conditions, they were often the victims of disease. The average life span of natives was only thirty-five years—about half that of other Americans.

A sharp contrast existed between the economic opportunities available to whites and natives. Natives "are not only undereducated for the modern world, but they are living where adequate education or training cannot be obtained, where there are few jobs, where little or no economic growth is taking place, and where little growth is forecast under present conditions." [30]

The Senate intended the land settlement to provide "a real

28. *Native Claims Settlement*, p. 99.
29. *Native Claims Settlement*, p. 100.
30. *Native Claims Settlement*, p. 100.

opportunity to break the chain of poverty which circumscribes their lives from birth, to bring needed services and public works to their home communities, and to develop their human and natural resources." That was the reason for granting money and giving natives control over their own financial institutions. "The basic purpose of the legislation," it was stated, "is to give Alaska natives the tools for making their own decisions, and the funds and expertise for carrying out their own programs." It could not be expected that the settlement would solve all the natives' problems at once, but it would go "a long way toward enabling the natives to construct the community facilities, develop the job opportunities, and obtain the training which are absolutely essential to maintenance of a viable society and economy in their villages." [31]

After four years of studying all aspects of the land problem, the Senate committee reported a "general consensus on the structural elements which constitute the settlement." It admitted that parties to the settlement—natives, the state, the federal government, and nonnative Alaskans—did not agree on all issues, and that all parties compromised to some extent. The law could be considered the last chapter in the history of the United States relations with Alaska's natives and one manifestly "just, generous, and honorable." [32] Signed into law by President Richard M. Nixon in December 1971, the measure extinguished aboriginal title in return for some forty million acres and almost one billion dollars. The act finally removed the cloud that native claims had cast on all land titles in Alaska.

In summary, the act entitled the natives to receive some forty million acres of land, including mineral rights; grants totaling $462.5 million from the federal treasury, payable over an eleven-year period, and some $500 million derived from an overriding 2 percent on the annual revenues from mineral leasing activity on state and federal lands. Twelve regional corporations (to which a thirteenth was added later, representing Alaska natives living out-of-state) and an estimated 220 village corporations control the land and monies granted to the natives under

31. *Native Claims Settlement,* pp. 105–106.
32. *Native Claims Settlement,* p. 106.

the act. The regional corporations are established under state law as business corporations, while the village corporations have the option of operating on a profit or nonprofit basis. Most, it appears, have preferred the business-for-profit form.[33]

Within two years of the enactment of the law, a roll of eligible persons was compiled who are members and shareholders of the corporations and who have a voice in management and a share in the lands, assets, and income of the corporations.[34]

The passage of the Alaska Native Claims Settlement Act (ANCSA) in 1971 coincided with the national concern over the environment. The gigantic projects planned for the North, including the Trans-Alaska Pipeline, focused the attention of national environmental protection organizations on Alaska. Their voices contributed to the delay of the construction permit for the Trans-Alaska Pipeline from Prudhoe Bay to Valdez and frustrated plans to build a large pulp mill and timber complex in southeastern Alaska. Environmentalist concern was important enough to require a trade-off in the passage of the ANCSA. That trade-off involved the withdrawal of some 80 million acres for possible inclusion in national parks, scenic and wild rivers, national forests, and wildlife refuges.

Today, as a result of the land-claim settlement, native corporations are investing in hotels, banks, fisheries, and other concerns. They are determined to provide two sometimes incompatible avenues to their people—economic self-sufficiency through involvement in industry, and the means of enjoying the traditional subsistence pattern of living for those who prefer it. While bargaining for a contract to maintain the North Slope Haul Road for the Alyeska Pipeline Company, they are opposing the state's road-building program, including opening the haul road to the public if it disrupts the familiar rural life.

The old image of dependent Alaskan natives hanging on somewhere between welfare and a subsistence economy has been altered radically by the claims settlement. One can only imagine the pleasure and pride among all natives when Roger Lang, executive director of the Alaska Federation of Natives,

33. U.S., *Statutes at Large*, 85 Stat. 688.
34. U.S., *Statutes at Large*, 85 Stat. 688.

made the fanciful offer to lend the state up to half a billion dollars to ease the economic crunch that will exist until North Slope oil begins to flow.

A sampling of native corporate projects reveals a diversity of investments. The Ahtna Corporation has contracted for the construction of pipeline camps and has invested in oil and gas exploration. The Aleut Corporation recently launched its first fishing boat, a 120-foot crabber-dragger. Another of these one-million-dollar vessels will be launched soon. Aleut has invested in real estate in Anchorage and is involved in hard-rock mineral exploration. The Arctic Slope Regional Corporation is building and remodeling commercial buildings in Anchorage, operating a heavy-equipment repair-and-maintenance garage in Barrow, engaging in the tourist and hotel business, and building residences. The Bering Strait Corporation purchased Pacific Alaska Airlines and has joined a Canadian firm to develop a mining operation and community at Fort River on the Seward Peninsula. It operates a trucking business and a tire-recapping enterprise, and plans house construction and a Norton Sound fishing co-op.

The Calista Corporation plans to build a 425-room hotel in Anchorage and has also invested $25-million joint venture for a recreational development at Settler's Bay, near Wasilla. Calista—a farsighted organization—has also founded a development corporation that will concentrate on environmental studies, industrial development, and earth protection. Along the way, Calista will do two hundred thousand man-hours of work on pipeline construction. Chugach Natives, Inc., has contracted to clear brush and prepare sites along the pipeline and handle lightering for cargo ships serving Valdez. Also in Valdez, the corporation contracted to provide oil-spill protection in the harbor.

Cook Inlet Region, Inc., has gone heavily into the hotel business. It now operates five hotels in Anchorage. Additionally, it will provide supplies and maintenance services to seven pipeline camps north of the Yukon River. Cook Inlet has entered the housing field, as well, and plans to build two hundred houses in the suburbs of Anchorage. Doyon, Ltd., which is headquartered in Fairbanks, has just built a $1.5-million office building for itself there and has a $14-million contract for the maintenance of the pipeline road north of the Yukon. Koniag, Inc., has purchased buildings in Kodiak, twenty-five fishing boats, and a fish-processing plant. The NANA Regional Corporation has a hotel at Kotzebue and a $15-million contract to provide security for northern pipeline camps. NANA will also invest in reindeer, in hopes of revitalizing that faltering industry. Finally, SeaAlaska is building an office complex in Juneau and is involved in timber management and marketing on the region's four hundred thousand acres of forested land.

Of course, some of these investments may prove unsound, and the more aggressive corporations may suffer from cash-flow problems. Several corporations have already been forced to borrow heavily to keep going. It is hoped, however, that the corporations will thrive, particularly as their management gains experience.

Their economic activity will benefit all Alaskans, but it does have a threatening aspect as well. Some of these developments could devastate the natural environment of Alaska. There is also a question concerning the future direction of native peoples under the impact of these commercial enterprises. Will it be possible to maintain and improve the rural culture in the face of the lure of employment in Anchorage and Fairbanks? We cannot predict with certainty what will happen, but a consideration of the natives' exposures in the past with poverty, oppression, and disease inclines one to be optimistic regarding their future.

14

Looking to the Future

WITHIN a few years of Vitus Bering's 1741 voyage of discovery, Russians began to exploit the resources of Alaska. The great value of sea-otter furs encouraged expansion and colonization on the continent of North America. Russian traders ignored the nominal claims of Spain to a territory the Iberians could not hope to develop or control. The Russians, originally as individual traders and later acting as a chartered company, strove to overcome the problems imposed by the expanse of the North Pacific and of the great land mass of northwestern North America. Merchants must pay profits to their backers, and that was possible only if the resources of Russian America could be exploited advantageously. In 1867, the Russians gave up. They had conquered native peoples but failed to overcome the tremendous impediments of Alaskan economic development, mainly climate, distances, and high transportation costs. The Russians were unable to develop agriculture or to tap any other resource to supplement the declining sea-otter wealth. Their administration of the natives showed little concern for the natives' well-being, and the Russians blundered in not building up the population.

Russian culture did not grip Alaska with long-lasting tenacity. Yet the American experience echoed that of Russia in the persistence of certain themes. The American government could not or would not govern to the satisfaction of Alaskans. It saw no

167

reason to induce settlement because of the expansiveness of its western frontier. It failed to stimulate agriculture or to manage the salmon fisheries intelligently. A lack of transportation, because of the nature of the country, handicapped development under American governance, although the Alaska Railroad and, later, the Alaskan Highway did provide some alternatives. Powerful forces persisted in retarding economic development, except when an Alaskan resource was in particular demand. The region's geographic location set it apart from the rest of the country and was responsible, to a great extent, for its slow economic pace. Yet a handicap can become an asset—a resource to be exploited at certain ripe times. That happened with Alaska's geography during World War II and subsequently. Military planners discovered the strategic significance of the top of the world and rushed troops and equipment to newly built bases. After the war, there was another flurry of activity when the construction of the Distant Early Warning Line seemed an urgent necessity. World War II was a watershed in Alaska's history. It stimulated more development in five years than had been sponsored over all the previous years of American possession. And, as always, the driving force was that of resource exploitation.

Alaskans cried out against the neglect and mismanagement of the federal government endlessly. Often enough, Congress and the federal bureaucracy believed that they treated the small populace and huge problems of the North with bountiful generosity and sympathetic understanding. Often that was true—but still Alaskans were convinced that the government was niggardly in filling needs and sometimes unaware of the richness of Alaskan natural resources. Alaskans felt that they were "managed" by forces beyond their control, that they were victims of squabbles among contesting federal agencies and conflicting national policies over resources that Alaskans needed to utilize. Alaskans insisted upon self-government. They were shocked to find that, when their goal was finally attained, it did not release them from the grip of federal agencies. The United States government still owned the vast majority of the land, as well as Alaska's expansive continental shelf. The federal government would continue to dictate the social and economic well-being of Alaskans by its management of the land. State policies on oil leasing cannot be based on a rational consideration of needs and priorities because of the competition of the Bureau of Land Management, which has been ordered to lease the outer continental shelf and explore Naval Petroleum Reserve No. 4 on the North Slope. The powerful international forces that determined the settlement of the Bering Sea fur-sealing dispute, a serious matter in the 1890s, are nothing like the forces that will dictate international oil policies. In the 1890s, some Alaskans complained that their fur-seal fishery regulation was determined by international diplomacy and manipulation. That was true; but statehood did not free Alaska from international oil politics. Every decision made concerning oil economics will affect Alaska. The state will be helpless before the giant movers and shakers of the oil world and subject to the vagaries of worldwide energy demands.

The state is clashing now with the federal government over competing land selections. Who will dictate the uses of forests and the selection of parks, reserves, wild rivers, and other restricted classes of land? Alaskans can voice their demands and carry them through the courts, but Alaskans remain a minute portion of the national population. National lands belong to all the people. Decisions will be made in Washington—a place where Alaskans do not enjoy heavy political clout.

When we tire of worrying about modern struggles over the land between familiar antagonists, we may agonize over a new clashing of interests. For many years, Alaskan natives petitioned the federal government for recognition of their rights to the land. Now natives possess selection opportunities. The pace of their selection and its thrust conflicts with the state's in some areas. That conflict and the need for money are dictating the state's policies. Natives will fight hard to achieve their ends. The litigation over the land among the natives, the state, and the federal government promises to be endless. As the old saying goes, only the lawyers will be happy. Ordinary taxpayers can only writhe in anticipation.

The conservationist-developer battles will continue to rage. Congress reacted to the energy crisis and a hope of gaining national self-sufficiency in petroleum by legislating the pipeline

construction, but other issues remain. Alaskans will feel they
are being interfered with, at times—but will not be able to avoid
interference. Other forces may, for example, dictate a wilderness park where the state wants coal mines. State residents can
focus their rage on the official who thwarts their intent, but that
will be small comfort. During an early resource-use dispute,
when the people of Cordova dumped coal from a dock in the
style of rebellious Boston "Indians" and burned an effigy of
U.S. Chief Forester Gifford Pinchot, no good resulted.
Then, as now, coal-land withdrawals could not be determined by
residents alone. Bumper stickers might help, psychologically.
During the 1972–1973 energy crisis, while the pipeline permit
was still held up in court, a popular sticker urged:

LET THE BASTARDS FREEZE IN THE DARK.

Another expressed a mixture of glee and frustration similarly:

FREEZING IN THE DARK BUILDS CHARACTER.

But dark humor does not obscure the emotional and intellec-
tual gap existing between conservationists and their opponents.
Alaskan miners were furious when Mount McKinley National
Park was created, and they are furious now at plans to enlarge
it.

Testimony taken in 1959 by a U.S. Senate committee considering the creation of an Arctic Wildlife Range in northeastern Alaska followed a familiar pattern. Alaskan miners were
the most strident opponents of the withdrawal of lands for the
range because they feared bureaucratic interference, despite the
fact that the bill did not exclude mining in the proposed range.
One witness argued that Alaska "stands now at the beginning of
a true and sound economic realization of her basic mineral resources." It would be foolish to hinder that development by
creating an unnecessary wildlife reserve. The new, struggling
state needed economic development badly. "We have had
enough of wilderness the past 50 years—it is time to guard
against too large a remainder at the end of another 50." [1]

1. U.S., Congress, Senate, Committee on Interstate and Foreign Commerce, *Arctic
Wildlife Range—Alaska Hearings,* 86th Cong., 1st sess., 1960, p. 259.

The arguments of the conservationists were just as cogent: "There is in this whole conservation movement an effort to make of the United States a Nation with the spiritual welfare of people one of its objectives. Many people, including a great number of Alaskans, are trying hard to make us human, in the best sense of that term." The conservationists went on to discusss the necessity to protect wildlife in large areas of Alaska because of climatic conditions. The spokesman was also pleased to report that the Tanana Valley Sportsmen's Association and other Alaskan sporting organizations supported the withdrawal of the land. That particular testimony—actually a letter published in the hearing record—ended the proceedings and, unsurprisingly, the uniqueness of Alaska was stressed. "Alaska has a unique opportunity in the world. So many people admire Alaska and like it for what it is, would like to go there. Let us not fill too much of it with the rubbish of industrialization." [2]

One witness, who was also speaker of the Alaska House of Representatives, complained of the "professional conservationists" who came from the Outside to intrigue in local matters. "I think they are quite a great interference in matters that should be strictly left to the people of the State of Alaska, and not be meddled into." That remark drew applause and groans from spectators, as did the remark that the animals of the Arctic that the speaker had observed were managing very well "under free enterprise." [3]

That witness was followed by another who spoke persuasively about the value of roads in the north. Roads were needed more than anything else. Lack of them constituted the greatest handicap to Alaskan development. Yet some people objected: "I don't understand their way of thinking at all, because we in Alaska have got to come up with something or we're going to be as bankrupt as our unemployment fund is, and it isn't very good for this winter's prospects." [4] Alaska could not be developed if land was denied to people. Everything was being closed up.

2. U.S., Congress, *Wildlife Range Hearings,* p. 456.
3. U.S., Congress, *Wildlife Range Hearings,* p. 247.
4. U.S., Congress, *Wildlife Range Hearings,* p. 232.

As might be expected, some indignant Alaskans have been seeking extreme political solutions to conditions of change that they deplore. They urge that Alaska become an independent nation and thus gain control over future events. A threat of secession does not seem to worry the rest of the United States greatly. But the lightly supported movement illustrates another old conflict among Alaskans: they desire their image as frontiersmen and want abundant, personally owned acreage surrounding their homes, yet most of them promote economic development as well. Economic development increases the population, fosters urban problems, and reduces the opportunity to own large tracts of land. It is not strange that people long for inconsistent goals.

Only the most reverent descendants of the Puritans who fled the Old World for the American wilderness could be upset to discover that their ancestors admitted to mixed motives for their migration. As one seventeenth-century pioneer in New England put it, succinctly, they came to praise God and make money. With a national heritage so firmly rooted in practical and spiritual aspirations, we should not wonder that migrants who have chosen to seek their fortunes in Alaska often reveal a mixed motivation that is somewhat contradictory in its goals. Newcomers to Alaska usually profess their interest in getting away from it all—and making money. Making money, as wags like to point out, usually involves the use of some of the "all" that the migrants wished to get away from.

A recent study of Alaskans shows that half the state's population resided outside Alaska five years earlier. The new Alaskans were not found to be indifferent or uncommitted to their new surroundings; on the contrary, they expressed a firm sense of identity with and loyalty to Alaska. What they found most attractive was the state's natural beauty and sparse population. Yet, according to the report, "Most Alaskans do not seem to want natural beauty preserved for its own sake and are interested in bringing as many settlers and tourists to the state as possible." [5] Development is not considered something ugly, but

5. Gordon Scott Harrison, *Alaska Public Policy* (Fairbanks: University of Alaska Press, 1971), p. 19.

rather the highest public and private good. So it is fair to paraphrase the goals of the Puritans: new Alaskans relocate in order to praise Nature and make money by exploiting it. And most of them plan to retire Outside.

Another problem for the state is the image of Alaska that is dominant in Washington, D.C. Alaskan economist George Rogers has pointed out that, historically, the official view of Alaska has been somewhat blurred. Bureaucrats accept a conception of Alaska that cannot be statistically described or physically identified. "From reading of official briefs, justifications, and testimony backing public policy decisions, this can be glimpsed in the form of certain stereotypes of Alaska as the 'last frontier' or some ideal formulation of what it is or should be." The view seems to be a reflection of "man's aspiration to create a better world and lead a more satisfying life in a corner of the great world of chaos and insanity." [6] That aspiration cannot be condemned, but it would be well if officials realized that 60 percent of Alaskans live in Anchorage and Fairbanks. Winter air pollution in Fairbanks surpasses that of Los Angeles, and the Alaskan city's sleazy, crime-ridden streets are no model for the world. From tall buildings and from the streets in Anchorage—a bustling metropolis rich in urban problems—nature-lovers can glimpse the magnificent Chugach Range; but otherwise, wilderness values there are negligible.

There is something unsporting about the insistence of some writers on the virtues of Alaska. "We now realize at what cost we have 'conquered' most of our continent," warned one authority. "Alaska today offers us something that history seldom affords—a second chance." [7] Such statements are nonsense, of course. There is no second chance in Alaska if there is none in California. Everywhere that men have lived and worked in Alaska, they have left the same clutter that is characteristic of the American life style. People who cannot maintain a pleasant countryside or city environs on the Outside could not be expected to do better with the "wilderness." The most important

6. George W. Rogers, *Future of Alaska* (Baltimore: Johns Hopkins Press, 1962), p. 18.

7. Paul Brooks, *Roadless Area* (New York: Knopf, 1964), p. 132.

industry for much of Alaska has been gold mining, and it was not an activity restricted to a few areas. There are countless areas where mining has long since been halted and where weeds and brush have made a determined comeback without effacing crumbling shanties, piles of tailings, and all kinds of rusting equipment. Cleaning it up would be a "second chance," and so would an effort to make Alaska's towns more attractive.

But first we must know what we are talking about. Reforms seldom proceed on ignorance. In the year of our pipeline boom, 1975, a respected *New York Times* syndicated columnist described the winter cold that "permeates the styles of all 350,000 Alaskans." [8] He then went on to describe the extreme cold of the interior and the Arctic coast as if all Alaska had the same type of climate. But from south to north, temperatures vary greatly. The *Times* authority did find something he thought promising in a most economical cold-climate method of building. In some instances, he tells us, the cold is put to use: watery mud, instead of costly cement, is poured around building foundations. Frozen within hours, it will hold the pilings firmly without rot for a few centuries. That is nonsense, of course, because permafrost, ground permanently frozen to a depth of up to a thousand feet, is the terror of a builder. Any solid structure exudes warmth. The warmth of any building based on permafrost without proper insulation would turn rock-hard ground into bottomless mud.

The state had successfully sold some 900 million dollars' worth of oil leases to various oil companies in 1969. In the afterglow of that big transaction, the state called for a conference of citizens to discuss directions for the future. Seminars were organized by the Brookings Institution, and a wide range of Alaskans participated in the meeting. On successive days, four different discussion groups examined the financial foundations for future Alaska, the use of human resources, and the quality of the natural environment. Throughout the sessions, there were repeated calls for a means of preserving "the Alaskan way of life." All participants seemed to have a feeling for the uniqueness of an Alaskan life style, and one group ventured a defi-

8. *Seattle Post-Intelligencer*, March 30, 1975.

nition: it is "a style that affords the conveniences of technological innovation combined with the opportunity and values of
living as close to nature as possible." [9] Most discussants
seemed certain that industrialization should be encouraged and
that proper regulation could preserve the balance that was necessary to the ideal life style. In short, Alaskan citizens agreed that
their state could enjoy the benefits of industry in a manner com-
patible with a close enjoyment of nature. Optimism reigned: "A
careful and schooled use of the oil resource wealth would excite
this life-style, adding a new dimension of opportunity. And it is
this opportunity that gives Alaskans a unique choice: they can
now, without doubt, build the mold for the future shape of the
state." [10]

In the seminar on future financial foundations for Alaska, the
citizens listed priorities. They called for flexible land classifica-
tion, environmental controls, an upgrading of the education system in rural areas, aid to communities lacking electric power
and sewage systems, improvement of mental health and more
effective treatment for alcoholism, and direct-revenue sharing
with local governments.

Discussions of the use of human resources focused on education, welfare, and concern for the aged. Participants insisted
that rural areas be provided with regional boarding schools so
that native children would no longer have to be sent Outside for
schooling. The need for bilingual education for natives was
stressed and the provision of a relevant curriculum was called
for. More vocational education, a greater emphasis on Alaskan
native history and culture, a more effective cultural-orientation
program for new teachers, and the encouragement of natives to
enter the teaching profession were other concerns on the citizens' list of needed reforms.

One group called upon the state to "guarantee and provide
for all its citizens a base level or minimum standard of living—
with particular attention to rural areas—in the fields of: health,

9. Brookings Institution, Advanced Study Program, in association with the Legislative Council of the State of Alaska, "A Conference on the Future of Alaska (Fall
1969)."

10. Brookings Institution Report.

sanitation, housing, education, employment assistance, entre-
preneurial assistance, senior citizens, mental health, alcoholism,
crippled children care, juvenile delinquency, family planning,
day care, and legal assistance.'' The language used in that and
other reports from these discussions was striking and betrayed
the strong humanistic leaning of the participants. They seemed
to be saying repeatedly—yes, we are going to be oil-rich, but
the money will be used to make life better for all Alaskans. The
importance of the provision of a minimum standard of living
was explained: ''A citizen has earned these minimum considerations because he is a *human being* and he is entitled thereby to
at least the opportunity to develop the talents within him—the
many talents which each of us possess.'' [11]

Speakers, outside experts in social-economic planning sponsored by the Brookings Institution, tried to warn the 150 ''representative'' Alaskans that they probably could not have their
cake and eat it, too. But the Alaskans resisted such cautions.
One speaker pointed out that 80 percent of Alaskans already
belong to the urban-technological society and that the changes
coming would destroy rural life styles, values, and the natural
environment itself. Alaskans have no choice, one lecturer
argued bleakly, for the forward march of the technological society is inevitable. No one has been able to determine the pattern
of urban-technological life. Can Alaskans do better? Can they
set their own priorities and translate these into policies? ''Yes,''
cried the discussants. ''Yes.'' Then they talked about the necessity of keeping the state's population low—while shouting
through a resolution that the Alaska Highway should be paved.

Current developments in Alaska are directly related to the
world petroleum market. After the Israel-Arab war of 1973 oil
prices quadrupled, and the Arabs threatened an embargo. President Richard M. Nixon reacted to the threat of an energy-supply
shortage by announcing a program through which the United
States could meet all of its energy needs by 1980. The primary
means of achieving that goal was to be the increased domestic
production of oil and gas. Thus the U.S. Department of the Interior was ordered to lease 10 million acres of the nation's outer

11. Brookings Institution Report.

continental shelf for petroleum exploration. No one is certain of the quantity of petroleum that may be produced, but extensive exploration in Alaskan waters has been going on for some years, and Interior officials believe that 50 billion barrels would be a reasonable guess.

After the initial uproar from conservationists and the state government over the proposed leasing, the Department of the Interior cut back on the acreage it had proposed to make available for development. In the Gulf of Alaska, 1.8 million acres, rather than the 3 million originally planned, would be leased. The reduction does not eliminate the environmental hazards, but Interior has also begun a five-year program of basic scientific environmental research, funded for 1974–1975 with $24 million.

Both the state and federal governments are planning leases of off-shore oil rights in the Beaufort Sea, Bering Sea, Chukchi Sea, Cook Inlet, and the Gulf of Alaska. Apparently there will be little controversy over the Beaufort Sea development, for there are no competing economic interests in that portion of the Arctic Ocean. But the conflict over leasing of the other areas is already under way and will be intensified. A high risk of environmental damage, particularly from oil spills, can be anticipated in waters that have yielded an abundance of fish and other sea products. The issues involved are more complex than was the dispute over granting Alyeska the Prudhoe Bay-Valdez pipeline permit. As Alaskan economist George Rogers put it: "We see here a confrontation between the world-wide energy crisis and the world-wide food crisis over which resources will ultimately have the higher value." [12]

As for the Gulf of Alaska, Alaskan fishermen have noted that its estimated annual sustained-yield harvest is over one million tons of food products. "Of primary importance is the amount of primary and secondary food production necessary to support fisheries' life. When compared with the Sea of Japan, Sea of Okhotsk and the Bering Sea, the Gulf of Alaska far and away

12. George W. Rogers, "Off-Shore Oil and Gas Developments in Alaska: Impacts and Conflicts," *Polar Record* 17, no. 108 (1974): 257.

produces more food benthos upon which fish feed, accounting for nearly 75% of the other three areas.'' [13]

Alaskans are also concerned about developmental risks in the Bering Sea and Bristol Bay. Governor Jay Hammond, once himself a Bristol Bay fisherman, has argued that the biological resources of the area might be more valuable than the petroleum resources. In 1972, the wholesale value of fishery products from Bristol Bay and the Bering Sea was nearly $1 billion. Fishermen of several nations earned $400 million for their catches in these prolific waters.

Competing economic values are not the sole consideration. Off-shore oil development will also have social implications. Fishermen will be forced out of business or face a reduced catch. Leasing of tracts under United States control will not bring any income to the state; yet the state and local communities will feel the impact of the activity. More schools, roads, and other services will be required for the influx of workers. At this writing, Alaska and other states in a similar predicament are pressuring the federal government for impact compensation, but the result is uncertain.

At the close of his long political-diplomatic career in 1869, William Henry Seward made a voyage around the world. His secretary's narrative of the journey is laced with reflections on the places visited and the people Seward encountered. Everywhere he saw signs of progress, because he was optimistic by temperament. Seward was certain that he had done well in acquiring Alaska for the United States. No one was better qualified to project Alaska's future than the man who was responsible for negotiating the purchase: ''Alaska—in the near future the great fishery, forest, and mineral storehouse of the world!'' [14] Soon after his prophecy was uttered, Alaska's fisheries began to yield their prolific bounty to the world, but the forests were not utilized until recent years and then only in a few limited regions of the southeastern Panhandle. As for the

13. Rogers, ''Off-Shore Oil and Gas,'' p. 257.
14. Oliver Risley Seward, *William H. Seward's Travels around the World* (New York: Appleton, 1873), pp. 35–36.

"mineral storehouse," miners scraped up goodly quantities of gold and copper within a reasonably short time of his forecast; yet there are quantities of other minerals, excluding petroleum, that have not been tapped. Still, on balance, we must give Seward high marks as an interpreter of the region's potential.

Another part of his description of Alaska is worthy of consideration. He referred to the Aleutian Islands as "hereafter to be the stepping-stones between the two continents" of North America and Asia. That perception of the destiny of the Aleutians as steppingstones has not yet been realized. In the heyday of the Russian-American fur trade, the islands filled that role much more effectively than they have at any time during the American period. Seward and others envisioned ships on the Great Circle route plying the North Pacific, calling at the islands for refueling and other purposes. Certainly that sometimes happened, but most passenger and freight ships held bunkers commodious enough to fuel their passage without losing time in the foggy, stormy waters of the chain. And although the Great Circle swings through the islands before arching to Japan, few skippers cared to sail north of the Aleutians. It has been much safer to keep to the south of the seas that have won deserved fame as producing the worst weather in the world.

If, however, we must discount Seward's vision on the basis of the Aleutians' history, we might err drastically in ignoring the possibilities of the future. The Bering Sea is likely to become one of the world's most important bodies of water in the near future. Petroleum prospectors are probing the shores and continental shelves of both the American and Siberian sectors and producing fields have been discovered. Assuming that cold-war tensions will continue to ease, it is not difficult to imagine the development of commercial traffic between the two continents. Even in an air-and-space age, it may be that the Aleutians will play a role beyond their current usage as wildfowl sanctuaries and military sites. Politics change, technology changes— but geographic actualities remain constant.

Ninety years after Seward described Alaska as the storehouse of the world, the same inspiration prompted President John F.

Kennedy. President Kennedy was more parochial—the storehouse was America's, rather than the world's, but otherwise the sentiments expressed by the two statesmen were the same:

> I see the Alaska of the future . . . I see an Alaska that is the storehouse of our nation, a great depository for minerals and lumber and fish, rich in waterpower and rich in the things that make life abundant for those who live in this great republic.[15]

The development of North Slope petroleum and the selection of land by the state and by native corporations are momentous events that should enable the storehouses described by Seward and Kennedy to begin to yield prodigiously. Insofar as they are able to control conditions, Alaskans must determine the best means.

15. Gruening, *State of Alaska*, p. 527.

15

Self-Views and Shabby Treatment

$\mathcal{N}$T is not easy to say whether Alaskans have been very different in attitudes or life styles from other Americans. Increasingly, since the turn of the century, Alaskan society has been overwhelmingly an urban one, and the pattern in town and city has not varied substantially from that set in other states. There are native villages where the traditional subsistence economy still predominates, but such an economy is becoming rare. For the most part, the state's residents cluster together and shop at Safeway and Woolworth's, rather than live off the land. Individuals who have seasonal employment in fishing, trapping, logging, and construction, however, do achieve something of a special life style.

Of course, it is possible to show that the predominance of urban conditions and familiar kinds of employment do not prevent the development of a unique character. That, at least, is what residents feel and express often enough. A perusal of the letters published in the *Alaska Magazine* supports that belief. In a recent issue, a writer insisted that "only here can one feel like and be an individual." [1]

The same letter column is usually full of praise of Alaska and

1. *Alaska Magazine*, November 1973, p. 24.

Alaskans from tourists who have found something compelling about the North. "It's difficult to explain to a person who has not been to Alaska," a man admitted. "All I know is that there is something that keeps drawing me back time after time." [2] In a similar vein, another writer explained that "the gist of my story was that you must experience the feeling of Alaska to really understand the Great Land. It creates an unshakable urge to return." [3]

The term *Outside* to designate any place except Alaska has been common for a long time. It does not seem incongruous today, even though air transportation has eliminated much of the isolation that existed earlier. Fairbanks is still fifteen hundred miles from Seattle, and northwestern Alaska is five thousand miles from Washington, D.C. Less frequently heard is the term *Outsider*. The tone of that term is invidious and suggestive of an Alaskan clannishness that does not actually exist. Most residents were Outsiders once, themselves, and left family and friends to whom they remain attached after moving north. Additionally, there is probably no state in the Union with so high a proportion of residents who leave permanently, once they are able to retire.

One Californian wrote to *Alaska Magazine* to object to the word *Outsider*. The writer was insulted and considered that, because residents had Alaskan license plates on their cars, they felt they owned Alaska. An Alaskan replied that he felt there was much more to being an Alaskan than having state license plates. Most Alaskans may have been Outsiders once, but "the point is they stayed . . . because they love the very ground they walk on." They take particular pride in the beauty of the land and the purity of the water "and they are caught up by the 'spirit'." That spirit is easily defined: it is one of independence, "the pure guts it took to sever all home ties and come here: the independence of a people building a state from the ground up and a pride in being part of the construction." Of course Alaskans act as if they owned the state. "They do! The true and proud Alaskans do own it. These people have built Alaska, have paid for it with sweat, mistakes, and more sweat. They love it,

2. *Alaska Magazine*, November 1973, p. 24.
3. *Alaska Magazine*, April 1973, p. 19.

curse it and dream about it but they also care about it." [4] Outsiders do not have the same attachment.

Another Alaskan writer pointed out that *Outsider* was never used in a hypercritical or derogatory manner—"it is simply a statement of fact." If Outsiders do not like the term, let them live at least a full year in Alaska. "I would like to see . . . [them] at 40 or 50 degrees below zero." [5]

Still another writer, who identified herself as a very new Alaskan, explained that Alaskans might get somewhat uptight with the influx of summer tourists, but insisted that as a traveler she had always found Alaskans friendly. She was also moved to declare her attitude: "I am proud to be among the 70 percent of Alaskans who have chosen to give up good jobs Outside, and to leave families and friends thousands of miles behind, in exchange for the privilege of living in this most beautiful and exciting of all the 50 states." [6] If visitors had a more positive attitude, they would not imagine that they hear Alaskans whispering behind their backs, she added.

Peoples' attitudes are conditioned to some extent by what they think themselves to be, whether they are in fact accurate in their appraisal or not. It is also true that people are affected by their view of their own past. There are several distinct interpretations of the history of Alaska. According to traditional accounts, the pioneers who joined the aboriginals in the North were sterling men and women who had to strive mightily to found their own communities. The odds against their achievements were enormous and their struggles unrelenting. They faced the severities of the most extreme winter climate of North America and had to learn how to adapt to it. Transportation—or, rather, the lack of it—was their chief hindrance. It was that and the vastness of the territory and its remoteness from the rest of the country that created the greatest hardship of all—the high prices set on everything imported from Outside. Virtually all food and goods had to be transported to Alaska. By comparison, other Americans lived easily and well.

4. *Alaska Magazine,* December 1973, p. 16.
5. *Alaska Magazine,* December 1973, p. 16.
6. *Alaska Magazine,* December 1973, p. 16.

If the story is a heroic one thus far, it becomes more so when we consider that there was a villain—in fact, two villains—in the piece. Of these, the first included all the transportation companies, suppliers, and various entrepreneurs who contributed to the high cost of Alaskan living. Most of the business interests were of Outside origin, but there were a handful of local business giants who were no less exploitive than the Outsiders. And, to spice the pot, the unnamed, unknown, pusillanimous investors who dared not venture into the Alaskan market would have to be added. If these timid moneymen had had sense enough to enter the field they could have driven prices down through their competition and speeded the progress of development by the injection of their capital.

The other villain—the greater one, because of the more ready identification and because it was an agency that was supposed to serve the interests of Alaskans—was the national government. A catalogue of its claims, omissions, stupidities, callousness, and neglect would stretch from here to infamy, from Barrow to Ketchikan. Why was the government such an ogre? Most Alaskans have agreed that the government had no evil intent but feel that their woes could be traced to the ignorance, indifference, and cowardice of bureaucrats. These three sins were enough to explain the problem. Alaskans suffered because the government lacked the courage to stand up to the special interests that exploited the resources of the territory without making any contribution of their own. They also suffered because, rather than placing knowledgeable Alaskans in key bureaucratic positions, the government preferred to put Outsiders, ignorant of Alaska and its problems, in charge of the territory's affairs. Politics rather than talent determined who would govern in Alaska. As historian Jeannette Paddock Nichols put it, Alaska "became a political preserve for the payment of small debts owed by big politicians to little ones." [7]

But did the government try to offset its timidity and callousness in these matters by fulfilling the needs and expectations of her northern citizens in other respects? Did it leap forward with vigor to provide the necessary basis of economic development? Most Alaskans would insist that the opposite was the case throughout the entire territorial history. During the emergencies of the gold rush and World War II, the government hacked out a few roads and trails—and one railroad to the interior—and did some construction, but there was no consistent effort to provide for obvious needs. Congress studied Alaska again and again—and subsidized countless junkets of its members and other office holders to the territory—but it never did carry out a master plan for systematic development. All right-thinking individuals realized that Alaska required a wide-scale, integrated transportation system, a careful survey of all its resource potential, and full encouragement of the development of that potential through direct or indirect support. It was as simple as that. No self-justifications of bureaucrats could obscure the story of neglect that retarded the region from the date of its acquisition in 1867 to its achievement of statehood in 1959. Ernest Gruening's history, *The State of Alaska,* labels several eras in terms that express the indictment well. He refers to "The Era of Total Neglect (1867–1884)," which was followed by "The Era of Flagrant Neglect from 1884–1898," and then conditions only improved a little with "The Era of Mild but Unenlightened Interest (1898–1912)." [8] Gruening, like the Alaskans of the period he wrote of, assumed that the government had the obligation of developing the territory, although the assumption was somewhat tenuous.

Yet the darker side of the government's infamy has not been told. Through all these years of ignorance, neglect, and indifference to both the atrocities of the exploiters and its own constitutional obligations, the federal government has denied the people of Alaska their basic political freedoms. Who spoke for Alaska? No one was designated for that role from 1867 until 1906. In 1906, the citizens were allowed to elect a delegate to Washington for the first time. Alaskans felt good about that progressive step, but they noted that the delegate was without power in the nation's capital. He could not vote on any of the vital legislation

8. Gruening, *State of Alaska*, pp. 11–12.

affecting Alaska or the country. The political subjection of Alaskans was not part of a conspiracy between government and special interests, although Alaskans were inclined to think so, at times. But even if the relegation of all Alaskans to a place of second-class citizenship is seen in the most favorable light, it still represents a scandalous and unwarranted proceeding. For long years, Alaskans called for justice, but their pleas were not heard. And though few in number, they could be loud. A certain exoticism lent strength to their pleas.

Little wonder, then, that the territory has been so tardy in its development. It is a wonder, too, that its people have been so patient, that they have been able to carry on their frontier lives with boldness and stamina in the face of all these impediments and have not resorted to rebellion.

The opposing or revisionist historical view is that Alaskans have raged irrationally against the reluctance of the government to grant self-government and that they have unjustly condemned the government for its scanty aid to economic development. Why should Alaskans have blamed the government for the slow growth of population that held back territorial organization and, later, state organization? All other regions of the country had to wait until their numbers aggregated to a reasonable level. Alaskans should have considered the other priorities of the nation in the late nineteenth and early twentieth centuries. At the time of the purchase of Alaska, the federal government was involved in all the problems of Reconstruction; then Americans had to settle the West, solve the money question, undergo an accelerated industrialization, and fight the Spanish-American War. The needs of a handful of whites in the North could hardly compete with those tasks—and should not have. Yet, despite the burdens of the nation, Alaska's needs were considered with the Organic Act of 1884, which provided for a district organization and, with the gold rush, a frenzy of federal activity was carried on to meet the demands of the huge and sudden influx of people. In retrospect, it would seem that Alaska got as much help as other territories and perhaps much more, in proportion, considering its small population.

Furthermore, certain assumptions of the traditionalists should be examined. It does not appear that growth was the immediate result of federal expenditures on developmental projects. The expensive Alaskan Railroad is a case in point. Its building did not spur immediate growth. Alaskans have been wrong in equating low development with sparse federal aid. Perhaps the thoughtless harping of Alaskans for more and more development has become an ingrained habit that could contribute to Alaska's destruction and even to the detriment of other parts of the world. It might be better to avoid development and preserve the scenic grandeur of the North, lest the mad pursuit of economic gain result in some vast environmental disaster, such as the damming of the Bering Strait or Arctic oil spills of tremendous proportions—two events that could alter the world's climate and create havoc on a large scale.

A review of traditional and antitraditional interpretations does not exhaust the list. Neither view pays more than passing attention to the historic treatment of native peoples. The following chronology is a summary from *Give or Take a Century* by Joseph E. Senungetuk:

1867: The Natives learn to their surprise that two foreign countries, having no title to their land, nor any rights to its resources, have bought and sold their entire property.

1884: Sheldon Jackson introduces a missionary system of education, a proselytizing system of religious teaching and practice.

1890: Protestant missionaries hold conference to allot and restrict areas of native education and Christian training to the various denominations.

1896–1899: Gold is discovered. . . . There is no regard and little respect for native land or resources.

1898: Native villages are left facing starvation, when a white teacher, William T. Loppe, directed a drive of 400 reindeer from Wales to Point Barrow to save the stranded crews of eight whaling vessels. The native economy collapsed.

1902: The school boards of Juneau and Ketchikan refuse Indian and Eskimo student enrollment.

1905: A dual educational and racist school system is set up by Congress for the Natives of Alaska.

1912: Alaska is made a Territory of the United States, but this has no effect upon the native peoples, who continue to live in poverty and disease.

1917: Alaskan natives again see an invasion of white prospectors searching for strategic minerals.

1930: Statistical reports reveal that the average annual income of an Eskimo family is between $300 [and] $500. Having replaced by force the satisfying subsistence economy of the native peoples, and thrust the population into an economy based on money, the Eskimos, Aleuts, and Indians were left to flounder in poverty. . . . There was not work for the native of Alaska.

1940–1953: The salmon runs continue to decrease, due to the large fisheries operating in Alaska by absentee owners in San Francisco and Seattle.[9]

Senungetuk's chronology goes on to trace the evaluation of native leadership and the first rounds of the settlement of native lands claims. His chronology holds errors of fact, but it is important as an expression of a particular interpretation that has much meaning. The traditional and antitraditional views are important for the same reason. They contain no factual errors, but are charged with misinterpretations, special pleading, and light attention to major economic, political, and social matters of great significance.

It is important that Alaska's past be understood as rationally as is possible. It is the usable past, as historian Jeannette Paddock Nichols has pointed out, that might provide some sound guidance for the future of Alaska. Historians should be challenged "to indicate wherein her past has, and has not, been useful to her." [10] If historians are able to do that, they might induce Alaska's leaders to cherish folklore less and historical truth more. Nichols condemned the persistent romanticism that has cast Alaskans "in the mold of perennial pioneers," because of the harm it does. "This kind of literary heritage," so persuasively presented by writers Jack London and Robert W. Service, "scarcely constituted a beckoning hand into the fu-

9. Joseph E. Senungetuk, *Give or Take a Century* (San Francisco: Indian Historian Press, 1971), pp. 217–218.

10. Jeannette Paddock Nichols, "Alaska's Search for a Usable Past," *Pacific Northwest Quarterly,* April 1968, p. 57.

ture.'' [11] Mrs. Nichols's strictures against nostalgia may seem harsh, and her approval of low attendance at a centennial gold-rush exhibit in Fairbanks may seem mystifying unless her argument is understood fully.

Probably the best approach to the past and future of Alaska is to observe the warnings of Mrs. Nichols and those of Alaskan economist George W. Rogers, who showed the confusion caused by the persistence of the ''last-frontier'' image in government. It is time enough now to think of Alaska as a place of rapid change—a change more momentous than any of those that have occurred in the past. I certainly agree with Mrs. Nichols that a true picture of past conditions and a rational consideration of current happenings can help to guide a rational development for the future.

11. Nichols, ''Alaska's Search,'' p. 59.

Suggestions For Further Reading

The shelves of many libraries, particularly those of federal record centers, groan under the weight of tons of documentary and manuscript sources of Alaskan history. Unfortunately, only a handful of scholars have delved into such treasure troves to unravel certain aspects of regional history. Much more work needs to be done before the place of Alaska in the national experience can be better understood. For the general reader, however, there are a number of fine published histories. These books can be divided into several categories: general history, native peoples, Russian America, and politics and events of the American era.

There are several major books available on Alaska's native peoples—coastal Indians, Aleuts, Eskimos, and Athabascans. Philip Drucker's *Indians of the Northwest Coast* (New York: American Museum of Natural History, 1963) discusses the Tlingit-Haida-Tsimshian cultures of the Panhandle. Erna Gunther has described the same cultures at the time of the initial white contact in the eighteenth century in *Indian Life on the Northwest Coast of North America* (Chicago: University of Chicago Press, 1972). Margaret Lantis has compiled a number of excellent essays in *Ethnohistory in Southwestern Alaska and the Southern Yukon, Method and Content* (Lexington: University Press of Kentucky, 1970). Eskimos have received more scholarly attention than other natives, and Wendell H. Oswalt's *Alaskan Eskimos* (San Francisco: Chandler, 1967) is one of the better assessments of their culture. Athabaskans (or Athapaskans), the predominant people of the Yukon basin, are the subject of a recent and well-written book by James Vanstone, *Athapaskan Adaptations* (Chicago: Aldine, 1974).

Hubert Bancroft's *Alaska* (1886; reprint edition, New York: Antiquarian, 1960) is still the best general history of the period

191

it embraces, 1730–1885. A 1945 publication, *Alaska: Promysh-lennik and Sourdough* (Norman: University of Oklahoma Press, 1945) by Stuart Ramsay Tompkins is another worthy general history that helps to fill some of the time lag since Bancroft. Alfred Hulse Brooks's *Blazing Alaska's Trails* (Fairbanks: University of Alaska Press, 1972) is a very good book by the former head of the U.S. Geological Survey in Alaska and one who knew the North intimately. Some historical errors mar the work slightly. Although primarily historical, the book also describes Alaska's climate, geology, vegetation, and animal life quite thoroughly. Brooks's personal observation of the early gold camps from Circle City to Nome enhances the value of the book.

Few scholars have delved into the Russian period of Alaska's history in any depth, but these few have produced some excellent work. Frank A. Golder's *Russian Expansion to the Pacific* (reprint edition, Gloucester: Peter Smith, 1960) and Hector Chevigny's biography of Aleksandr Baranov, *Lord of Alaska* (New York: Viking, 1942) are good examples. The hard-driving and colorful Baranov was the first governor of the Russian-American Company. S. B. Okun's *Russian-American Company* (Cambridge: Harvard, 1951) is useful but is not a very comprehensive study of the great trading enterprise. More recently, a Russian scholar has written a valuable book: Svetlana Fedorova's *Russian Population in Alaska and California From the Late 18th Century to 1867* (Kingston, Ontario: Limestone Press, 1973). Still another study by a Russian is *Russians on the Pacific, 1743–1799* (Kingston, Ontario: Limestone Press, 1975) written by Raisa V. Makarova.

Alaskan history of the American era is not illuminated by more than a few landmarks of distinction. Jeannette Paddock Nichols's *Alaska: A History* (1924; reprint edition, New York: Russell and Russell, 1963) focuses on the first fifty years of American rule with care and perception. Ernest Gruening's *State of Alaska* (New York: Random House, 1968) is the only other general political history of any note. Both of these writers accuse the federal government of having neglected Alaska. Official efforts to put Alaska on the map are detailed in Morgan

Sherwood's lively *Army Exploration in Alaska* (New Haven: Yale University Press, 1965). Ted C. Hinckley has written an excellent account of *The Americanization of Alaska, 1867–1897* (Palo Alto: Pacific Books, Publishers, 1972) and Claus-M. Naske's *An Intrepretative History of Alaskan Statehood* (Anchorage: Alaska Northwest Publishing Company, 1973) is an excellent treatment of the Alaskan achievement of political maturity.

The only World War II military campaign fought on American soil was that on the Aleutian Islands. Though the battle did not win much glory for either combatant, it has its interest and has been described superbly by Brian Garfield in *The Thousand-Mile War* (New York: Doubleday, 1969).

The author has written a social history of the gold era, *North of 53°: The Wild Days of the Alaska-Yukon Mining Frontier* (New York: Macmillan Publishing Company, 1974) and has also examined the Bering Sea frontier in *Arctic Passage: The Turbulent History of the Land and Peoples of the Bering Sea, 1697–1975* (New York: Charles Scribner's Sons, 1975).

Index